Third-Wave Cognitive T
Treatment of Loss and (

This book proposes and explores a novel conceptualisation of the grieving process grounded in evolutionary psychology that integrates cognitive behavioural approaches such as compassion focused therapy, metacognitive awareness, and acceptance and commitment therapy.

Starting with an introduction of the historical and theoretical basis for the Principles of Loss model, the book then outlines methods of assessment and describes the processes of formulation and case conceptualisation, with specific guidance on how to navigate these in the context of loss. The book provides an in-depth exploration of the Five-Phase Principles for the Treatment of Loss and Grief (intervention), as well as guidance on the supervision of loss. The chapters, accompanied by case studies, provide an overview of the novel model, followed by specific and tailor-made guidance on assessment (including a novel self-report measure), formulation, treatment, and supervision.

This guide is intended for clinicians familiar with or interested in the theory and practice of third-wave cognitive behavioural therapies.

Faramarz Hashempour, PhD, is a consultant psychotherapist who is an accredited practitioner, trainer, and supervisor with the BABCP. He is also an EMDR consultant working across the UK, Ireland, and Europe. Faramarz has a background in research and teaching diversity and symbolism. He has a working career in adults, forensic psychiatry, children and young people. He is currently working in his own independent practice.

Navya Anand, DClinPsy, is a clinical psychologist trained in third-wave cognitive behavioural therapies and systemic approaches. Her work is grounded in social constructionism and focuses on the interactions between power, privilege, and identity. She currently works as an academic tutor with the clinical psychology training course at the University of East London.

'In the past few years many people have died due to COVID-19 and instead of being able to follow our traditions, cultures and faiths about death and dying, people across the world were forced to change these vital processes. I personally believe that the changing of these essential rites of passage has and will have a profound impact on the grieving process and thus on people's mental health in general. I have found this book to be clearly written, very engaging and right now so needed by students, clinicians, educators and researchers as the issues with complex grief are going to be on a scale never seen before. I am delighted to recommend this text.'

– *Derek McLaughlin, PhD, RN*, *Senior Lecturer and Professional Lead for Mental Health Nursing, Queen's University Belfast*

'A Turkish saying goes, "The journey of those without a guide ends in a dead end." In a difficult clinical field such as complicated grief, where the therapeutic process can be injurious for clients as well as ambiguous for clinicians, the authors offer us a valuable guide in which clinical practice is built on a strong theoretical model and embodied in case vignettes.'

– *Vahdet Gormez, MD, MRCPsych*, *Associate Professor and Chair, Department of Child and Youth Mental Health, Istanbul Medeniyet University*

'Without question the authors have created the definitive guide for working effectively with grief and loss. The guide provides valuable clinical insights on assessment, formulation and case conceptualisation through to how to implement the five-phase protocol in your practice and is enhanced with clinical examples throughout. An essential text.'

– *Marie Chellingsworth, Founder, The CBT Resource and Senior Lecturer*

Third-Wave Cognitive Therapy for the Treatment of Loss and Grief

A Clinician's Guide

Faramarz Hashempour and
Navya Anand

Routledge
Taylor & Francis Group

LONDON AND NEW YORK

Designed cover image: Cassia Roxanna Hashempour

First published 2023
by Routledge
4 Park Square, Milton Park, Abingdon, Oxon OX14 4RN

and by Routledge
605 Third Avenue, New York, NY 10158

Routledge is an imprint of the Taylor & Francis Group, an informa business

British Library Cataloguing-in-Publication Data
A catalogue record for this book is available from the British Library

Library of Congress Cataloging-in-Publication Data
Names: Hashempour, Faramarz, author. | Anand, Navya, author.
Title: Third-wave cognitive therapy for the treatment of loss and grief :
a clinician's guide / Faramarz Hashempour & Navya Anand.
Description: Abingdon, Oxon ; New York, NY : Routledge, 2023. |
Includes bibliographical references and index.
Identifiers: LCCN 2022032277 (print) | LCCN 2022032278 (ebook) |
ISBN 9781032101774 (hbk) | ISBN 9781032101750 (pbk) | ISBN 9781003214045 (ebk)
Subjects: LCSH: Grief therapy. | Loss (Psychology) | Cognitive therapy. |
Acceptance and commitment therapy.
Classification: LCC RC455.4.L67 H37 2023 (print) |
LCC RC455.4.L67 (ebook) | DDC 616.89/1425–dc23/eng/20220923
LC record available at https://lccn.loc.gov/2022032277
LC ebook record available at https://lccn.loc.gov/2022032278

ISBN: 9781032101774 (hbk)
ISBN: 9781032101750 (pbk)
ISBN: 9781003214045 (ebk)

DOI: 10.4324/9781003214045

Typeset in Helvetica
by Newgen Publishing UK

Contents

Figures

Tables

Chapter 1

Introduction

Loss, Grief, and Mourning

It is natural and inevitable that humans experience loss; whether this is the loss of a loved one, a relationship, a job, or a role – the dynamic nature of life ensures that we all must confront loss and, to some extent, overcome it. Loss is an episode: a moment or event in which something is removed from one's life. Grief encapsulates the affective, cognitive, and value-based processes that occur due to loss. Bereavement is the overarching process of coming to terms with loss. The experience of loss and the subsequent internal processing of that loss follow highly similar trajectories across cultures; grieving is an intrinsic mechanism by which all humans are able to recognise, identify, and assimilate the loss. The behaviours that an individual expresses in relation to this process of grief, however, vary across cultures; mourning behaviours are socially constructed, with some behaviours being "socially acceptable" in some cultures and not in others based on culturally, religiously, or philosophically driven values and practices – hence creating a variety in mourning, whilst the inherent experiences of loss and grief remain the same.

The extent to which the lost object – object here referring to any internal representation of what is lost, whether that be a person, a relationship, or a role – is valued or intrinsic to the individual determines their response in the aftermath of the loss. The ways in which the individual copes with the loss, and the extent to which these methods are "successful" (i.e. the extent to which the person is able to continue with functioning) depend on the individual's cognitive and affective approaches to difficulty. This includes their metacognitive style, the amount of self-compassion they are able to practice, and their previously used coping strategies.

For some individuals, the loss is valued so highly, and interacts with others factors such as their perceived ability to cope and the manner of the loss (e.g. traumatic bereavement due to suicide), that the grief response becomes prolonged and intensified. This is referred to as complicated grief and has been known to self-perpetuate until external help is provided.

DOI: 10.4324/9781003214045-1

Whereas individuals experiencing typical grief do not require psycho-therapeutic intervention, those experiencing complicated grief benefit greatly from therapy. However, existing models of grief and complicated grief, as well as existing therapeutic approaches are based on antiquated conceptualisations and models. This book aims to delineate a theoretical and therapeutic approach to complicated grief based on a novel integration of third-wave cognitive behavioural therapy (CBT) approaches that is rooted in evolutionary theory.

This book aims to introduce and explore an innovative approach in the treatment of complicated grief that conceptualises loss as a natural experience and grief as an evolutionarily developed process. In order for us to gain a better understanding of how this process evolved, we will take a look at past understandings of the concept of grief, reflect on theoretical positions, and finally offer a novel route to assessment, formulation, and intervention. To begin with, we turn briefly to historical perspectives, where we can note the changes in understanding and treatment of grief and better management of loss over the course of history.

Historical Perspective

Throughout antiquity, humanity has had to deal with a number of losses through hardship of environment, resources, materials, and loved ones. Loss has been grieved, and grief has been displayed in acts of mourning – albeit in varying ways over the millennia of human existence. Oftentimes, emotional processing of the loss (grief) and its communication (mourning) occurred as part of rituals, music, and laments – therefore grieving was an outward-focused activity that conveyed one's distress to others, as opposed to an inward-looking process relating to one's ways of coping with the loss emotionally. The earliest record of mourning comes from the *Epic of Gilgamesh*, written over 4000 years ago in ancient Mesopotamia; King Gilgamesh upon losing his closest friend and ally states "I shriek in anguish like a mourner" and that "All mourn you; the weeping does not end day or night". Gilgamesh replaces his royal apparel with the skins of wild animals, and wanders into the wilderness – demonstrating outwardly with his behaviour, the inward confusion and turmoil he is experiencing following his loss.

Almost 1000 years after the Sumerian/Akkadian *Epic of Gilgamesh* was written, came the *Iliad*. Written by Homer in ancient Greece in the 12th century BCE, the *Iliad* follows the Trojan War, with Achilles as the hero. In the *Iliad*, Achilles experiences undeniable grief when he loses his close friend and comrade Patroclus; he is distraught: "the black cloud of sorrow closed on Achilles./ In both hands he caught up the grimy dust, and poured it/over his head and face… tore at his hair with his hands, and defiled it… he himself… in the dust lay". As in Gilgamesh, Achilles demonstrates his inner disquiet through outward changes in his behaviour and appearance. Onlookers mourn with Achilles, and lament the loss together – demonstrating this by beating their chests with their hands and crying out. Although formal mourning rituals existed at the time that the Iliad was written and are incorporated in the epic elsewhere (e.g. "thrênos", a lament that is written and performed by professional mourners), it is Achilles' pure unadulterated pain and sorrow that leads him to make such a public display of his grief ("góos"), and which is so powerful that those around him "mourned with him, letting the tears fall".

The tendency to use behavioural, social, ritualistic processes to demonstrate and assuage a person's grief is a long-standing tradition that continued well into the 5th century BCE. It is from this time that we first have sources describing a *verbal* treatment for grief focused on one's internal states, as opposed to a *behavioural* ritual focused on socially demonstrating loss. Antiphon is credited with this change in stance; he advertised his "method for the cure of grief… through the power of words". He was an orator and educator, delivering "grief-assuaging lectures" to the people of Athens. This shift towards developing a language for the internal states of the mind in order to convey the turmoil of grief has continued since the time of Antiphon into modernity. When studying the works of Cicero (his *Letters*, *Consolation to Himself*, and *Tusculan Discussions*), who was writing in the first-century BCE, we can see the process of his grief playing out in his words. Cicero lost his public political status at the end of the Republic, his wife to divorce, and his daughter passed away during childbirth – with all three events occurring in close succession. Unsurprisingly, these losses had an immense impact on Cicero. His *Letters*, written to a close friend, depict the immediate and acute grief following loss. We see him struggling with the raw pain of his grief as he states "I am so overcome with tears that I can not bear up"; "I have nothing, in which I can find peace… Now I reject everything and find nothing to be more bearable than solitude". Finding that his emotional pain was not abating, Cicero took to reading all that he could find on the subject of grief; unfortunately, given the "stiff upper lip" attitudes prevalent at the time – "others want me to hide the depth of my grief" – especially for those of high social and political status such as Cicero, he was not able to find anything particularly helpful in managing his own grief. Due to this, Cicero, using his oratory skills of persuasion and reason, writes a *Consolation to Himself* – a speech intended to persuade him out of his own grief. It is perhaps the first recorded instance of an individual attempting to reason with their emotions, and to alter their perspective on their losses in order to move forwards in life. He attempts to reframe his emotional pain by turning inward his skill of oration and persuasion – and perhaps he intends this to be used by others who are bereaved to help them manage their grief. Finally, in *Tusculan Discussions*, Cicero shifts towards a broader acceptance-based philosophical standpoint; he must place his grief within the wider frame of life in order to understand the impact of these losses for him, and how he can continue his life in spite of these experiences.

This gradual shift in the use of performative rituals to demonstrate grief in a socially acceptable manner, to the use of introspection and language to process one's inner grief – as well as convey it to those closest – is evident in the greatest literary works throughout the ages. Jumping forward in time to the 16th-century CE, we see this tradition in the works of Shakespeare. It is in his tragedies that we can see most clearly losses, their impact, grief, and mourning as experienced by Shakespeare's characters. *King Lear*, following the loss of his kingdom, his social network, and betrayal by his elder daughters states "I am bound/Upon a wheel of fire, that mine own tears/Do scald like molten lead". When Lear's favoured youngest daughter dies, he is distraught: "Howl, howl, howl, howl! ... I might have sav'd her; now she's gone for ever!". Similarly in *Hamlet*, the play begins shortly following the death of the King, and his son – Hamlet II – is grieving his loss still. Hamlet states "'Tis not alone my inky cloak... suits of solemn black... the fruitful river in the eye... Together with all forms, modes, shows of grief". Towards the end of the play, when Hamlet learns of the death of his beloved Opehlia, he is distraught, stating that he would "weep... fight... fast... tear thyself... Be buried quick with her" in his anguish.

We see here a slow shift from non-emotional, ritualistic processes to mark a loss, towards an emotional vocabulary that enables the bereaved to express the depth of their grief in words that others around them can comprehend. Although the perspective seen in the works of Antiphon and Cicero is not necessarily present in the performative works of Shakespeare, a paradigm shift has occurred; by the time we meet Bowlby and Freud in the 19th-century CE, there are clear social narratives about the ways in which grief can be experienced and expressed. Bowlby links his attachment theories to the experience of loss – contributing to a growing understanding of the importance of looking intrapsychically when working with grief. Furthering this, Freud in his seminal work "Mourning and Melancholia" sets the tone for all psychological research to come; he differentiates between "normal" and "atypical" responses to loss – a distinction that we continue to see today in the term "complicated grief".

What we can see when we take a historical perspective is that all humans experience loss and all humans grieve; the manner in which this grief is expressed, as mourning, may differ across time, geographical region, and culture – but the fact of grieving remains universal. It is merely the way in which grief is conceptualised and theorised which has changed over time, as well as the support that is available and accessed by those in mourning. Some cultures and religions continue to hold elaborate funeral rites and rituals to mark a loss, and the ways in which mourners are able to express their grief differs in these different settings. For example, in certain

Hindu communities the funeral rites are 12 days in length, with hundreds of family and friends visiting the bereaved family to pay their respects. The bereaved are largely expected to contain their grief and to "put on a brave face" – especially the men in the family. There is often so much to arrange during the funeral period that family members do not have time to process the emotional impact of the loss. Another instance of note relates to some Islamic communities where there is a disparity between those who wish to mourn through expressive grief (beating their chests, crying, scratching the face) and those who follow a more constrained response to "let go" or "move on" in the immediate aftermath of the loss. Thus a contrast exists between what is socially acceptable in some cultures and communities but not in others; however, the fact of loss and grieving remains the same. It is merely the ways in which this grief can or cannot be expressed, and the extent to which mourners have access to social support in the aftermath of the loss that varies across cultures and contexts.

Although loss does not only relate to death, this is a common occurrence that all of us must endure within our lifetimes. In modern contexts, when we lose a person, we do not only lose the connection that we had with them, but also their knowledges, wisdoms, support, and their economic power – to name but a few of the facets of loss. Human societies are built on social networks and interconnectedness. Regardless of whether one hails from a "collectivist" or "individualistic" society, people need people (Triandis, 2018). Whether that is for emotional, physical, social, vocational, or financial support; no person is an island. Therefore losing someone from that social network brings certain impacts for the different people in that network. Those whose lives were more intrinsically bound to the life of the deceased are likely to be most affected by the loss, as they stand to lose the most from the absence of that individual – whether that loss manifests as a lack of financial support, moral support, or emotional support is irrelevant. The greater the role the deceased had in your life, the greater the loss is for you – and the greater the impact on your life and your ability to function thereafter. For example, if you are reliant on one person for the majority of an income that supports your livelihood, then it is clear that losing that person would be devastating for you emotionally and financially. Adding the financial burden element on top of the emotional pain of the loss is likely to complicate the grief that is experienced, and perhaps prolong the dysfunction that occurs following the bereavement.

It is notable that in spite of the fact that we are all different in our cultures, from the evolutionary point of view we do have some similarities; in other words, the mechanics of the grieving process is almost identical for us as human beings. Where we differ however is in areas such as our understanding of the loss, our knowledge, cultural stance, spiritual views, or philosophical position. These are some of the contributory factors that have provided us with a different mode of coping, resilience, and other supportive resources in combating the experience of loss and its impact on us. The following section of this chapter provides an overview of existing theoretical and therapeutic models of grief. Following this, we provide an introduction to our model: a novel integration of third-wave cognitive behavioural therapeutic approaches to grief.

Theoretical Position

Death is the natural and inevitable conclusion of human life, yet the experience of loss, the process of grieving, and the experiences of the bereaved remain incredibly varied, idiosyncratic, and at times – elusive. Theorists and clinicians alike have attempted, for the better part of 100 years, to describe and explain the process by which humans grieve. The understanding and management of grief have been characterised by the identification of a disparity between "normal" and "complicated" grief. The majority of models of grief have centred on stage- or phase-based approaches that delineate the trajectories that grief takes, with an explicit focus on the symptoms that arise.

Although such approaches are long-standing and well-established, they have not been updated with more recent empirical evidence and theoretical and therapeutic advancements in the field of psychotherapy. The main omissions of these models are values-based conceptualisations and an understanding of the impact of loss on an individual's functionality. We propose a novel approach that views grief from an evolutionary perspective, focuses explicitly on the functional impact of loss, and integrates third-wave cognitive behavioural approaches to provide an up-to-date theoretical and therapeutic model.

Previous Conceptualisations of Grief

Loss does not only relate to the death of loved ones – therefore a caveat is required at the start of this section. The majority of work on grief has focused on the experiences of people who have been bereaved, and there is a lack of available models that conceptualise loss and grief from a broader perspective. Due to this, the following section focuses mainly on grief as a result of death; our model presented later in this chapter does not limit grieving to mortality, as it expands on the importance of considering losses beyond death. We acknowledge the shortcomings of focusing exclusively on death as a form of loss, and hope that the content of this book will be useful for other forms of loss that clinicians may encounter in their practice.

Young et al. (2012) outline three categories of grief: acute grief, integrated grief, and complicated grief. They suggest that acute grief is characterised by numbness, shock, and denial immediately following loss; this is a natural and necessary response that over time gives way to the experience of challenging emotions such as pain, sadness, and emptiness. The intensity of these emotional experiences reduces over time. In the majority of cases, this acute grieving phase naturally transitions into integrated grief which is characterised by recognition of the process of bereavement, being able to think about the deceased, being able to re-engage with socio-occupational functioning, to re-connect with others, and to experience pleasure once again.

In approximately 7% of individuals who experience a loss, acute grief does not naturally resolve into integrated grief (Simon, 2013): the acute grief becomes prolonged, causes significant distress, and impairs socio-occupational functioning; this is termed as "complicated grief." Generally speaking, normal grief involves a series of stages or phases (not necessarily in a given order), that shift the individual from their initial shock and intense negative experiences of the loss, towards a more regulated state of functioning in which a continued relationship with the deceased is forged (Hall, 2014). Conversely, complicated grief is characterised by prolonged grief responses, a lack of resolution of the grief, trauma-like symptoms, and persistent impairment in socio-occupational functioning (Howarth, 2011). Research suggests that psychotherapeutic interventions are both necessary and beneficial for individuals experiencing complicated grief (including traumatic bereavement), whereas such intervention is neither necessary nor useful for individuals experiencing typical grief (Neimeyer, 2000). Although complicated grief has not formally been recognised as a distinct diagnostic category in the Diagnostic and Statistical Manual (APA, 2013), it remains a presentation that has often been documented across many decades of clinical and empirical work. Given this, it is likely to be useful to distinguish between typical and atypical (i.e. complicated) grief when planning and undertaking psychological intervention. Therefore, the remainder of this guide continues to make the distinction between normal and complicated grief, whilst acknowledging the lack of formal diagnostic criteria – and suggesting that diagnostic labels are neither necessary nor sufficient when working clinically with grief. Rather than basing intervention on the existence of a formal diagnostic label, we suggest that clinicians focus on the idiosyncratic functional impairment caused by loss in order to work meaningfully with grief.

A plethora of research addresses the nature of normal and complicated grief; the extrinsic factors that lead to one and not the other; idiosyncratic factors that influence the process of grieving; the ways in which to support individuals such that their complicated grief is converted into normal grief – the list is endless. Hall (2014) provides a comprehensive overview of the development of grief theories over time, as summarised here. Models of grief began with Freud (1957), who outlined three stages of the normal grieving process: (1) freeing the bereaved from the deceased;

(2) readjusting to a new life without the deceased; and (3) building new relationships. He placed emphasis on the need for acknowledging and expressing difficult emotions in therapy, as a way of achieving a cathartic shift in one's relationship to the deceased. Bowlby (1963) extended this when he conceptualised complicated grief as yearning for the lost object, experiencing anger towards the lost object and also towards the self, caring for others in a compulsive manner, and denying permanent loss. These nebulous concepts were crystallised by Kubler-Ross (1969). Kubler-Ross (1969) developed a five-stage (predictable) model of grief: denial, anger, bargaining, depression, and acceptance. Kubler-Ross implied that failing to move through these stages in this order would result in complications. Whilst this model remained popular for decades and became integrated with lay conceptions of grief (as seen, e.g., in an episode of the TV show The Simpsons), it has since been criticised in academic circles and empirically rejected. Later approaches favoured phase-based theories. For example, Rubin et al. (2009) developed the two-track model of bereavement involving the outcome of the loss (biopsychosocial responses to bereavement) and the relational bond (transforming the attachment to the deceased, and forming an ongoing relationship with the deceased). Similarly, Schut (1999) proposed the dual process model of bereavement, which involves oscillation between: (1) loss orientation (emotion-focused coping, internal focus) and (2) restoration orientation (problem-focused coping, external focus). Moving between these two processes is seen to be a necessary part of the grieving process, rather than being interpreted as pathological avoidance or denial.

By the early 21st century, a new shift occurred: trajectory-based conceptualisations of grief became popular. Bonanno et al. (2002) outlined five grief trajectories: (1) common grief; (2) stable low distress; (3) depression then improvement; (4) chronic grief; and (5) chronic depression. The distinction between chronic grief and chronic depression lies in the cognitive processes; chronic grief is characterised by increased processing of the loss and greater search for meaning whereas chronic depression is not. This reflected a wider shift in the field towards narrative approaches, as the idea of severing bonds with the deceased gradually changed into the concept of maintaining bonds with the deceased (Klass et al., 2014). As Hall (2014) describes, the focus of "grief work" shifted from separating the bereaved from the deceased, to finding and understanding the meaning of the loss, and processing the meaning in an idiosyncratic and adaptive manner in order to allow the bereaved to re-engage with their life. More recent theories have also shifted backwards in terms of model type, such as Worden (2018)'s task-based model. Worden suggests that grieving is an active process involving four major tasks: (1) accept the loss; (2) process the pain; (3) adjust to a new life without the deceased; and (4) find an enduring connection with the lost object whilst continuing new life. Worden suggests that the following factors affect the individual's experience – both risk-related and protective: (1) relation to deceased; (2) attachment to deceased; (3) manner of death; (4) historical antecedents; (5) personality; (6) social mediators; and (7) stressors simultaneously present. Worden's is the first theoretical model that attempts to explain the distinction between normal and complicated grief in a quantifiable manner. He proposes factors that contribute to the development of complicated grief as opposed to normal grief and provides a non-linear model that outlines the emotional and social processes that need to occur for complete processing of loss.

Cognitive Behavioural Approaches

Despite all of this, what is clear from the literature is that we do not know the mechanisms or processes of grief much better than the first theorists such as Freud and Bowlby. There have been various attempts to apply theory to practice, and multiple therapeutic approaches aimed at helping those with complicated bereavements to "successfully" grieve their losses and re-engage with their lives. These approaches have often been contradictory – for example, in the 1970s, the focus of therapy was on breaking the bonds with the deceased in order to allow the bereaved to continue with their lives. On the other hand, in the 1990s, the emphasis of therapy was to build continuing bonds with the deceased in order for the bereaved to fully process the loss (Malkinson, 2010). Here we see starkly the trial-and-error nature of the work that has been conducted to date. A major unspoken assumption within all of these theoretical models seems to be encapsulated by the idiom "time heals all wounds"; there is an assumption that given sufficient time, individuals naturally progress from complicated into normal grief, and hence are able to process their loss fully. However, this has been shown not to be the case. The death of someone significant is associated with increased risk of mortality in the deceased – no matter the time allowed for grieving to occur – suggesting that it is not the amount of time, but the quality of that time (i.e. the way in which the loss is processed) that determines the outcome of the bereavement (Rostila & Saarela, 2011).

Given that time does not heal all wounds – and certainly not the wound of loss – it has been suggested that the CBT approach (Beck, 1979) may be appropriate when working with individuals experiencing prolonged and/or complicated bereavement. The CBT approach is both widely used and well-evidenced; a corpus of quantitative research attests to its effectiveness at the population level, leading to an increase in the provision of CBT for the treatment of common mental health conditions in the UK (e.g. in Improving Access to Psychological Therapies [IAPT] services). Additionally, CBT is already in use as a form of treatment for complicated grief – albeit without the modifications necessary for targeting grief-specific symptoms.

Current uses of CBT for the treatment of grief are limited to the use of post-traumatic stress disorder (PTSD) models of CBT (Ehlers & Clark, 2000) for the treatment of traumatic grief – which is a form of complicated grief resulting from death by traumatic or unexpected means (Howarth, 2011), the use of complicated grief therapy (CGT; Malkinson, 2007, 2010; Malkinson et al., 2006) which has a foundation in both CBT for PTSD and interpersonal psychotherapy (IPT) for depression (Wetherell, 2012), and CBT-based self-help approaches such as the *Overcoming Grief* book by Sue Morris (2018).

CGT is a 16-session protocol that has been empirically tested in various randomised controlled trials (RCTs), which is the "in vogue" methodology of choice in modern psychology (e.g. Shear et al., 2005; Shear et al., 2016; Shear et al., 2014). Shear et al. (2001) outline the methodology used in CGT as follows: this approach aims to reduce the intensity of grief, increase pleasant memories of the deceased, and encourage re-engagement with one's social network and activities of daily living. In CGT, reduction of the intensity of grief is achieved through imaginal and in vivo graded exposure tasks, which are intended to reduce avoidance behaviours. Imaginal reliving is used to identify hotspots (as in CBT for PTSD), and exposure is conducted both in session and as part of homework. IPT techniques are used to help bereaved individuals reconnect with their socio-occupational functioning.

Whilst CGT appears to be an effective treatment for complicated grief, further research is required in order to establish its effectiveness. RCTs are useful for demonstrating efficacy (internal validity within highly controlled research environments), and results seldom generalise well when treatments are applied in typical clinical settings (Carey & Stiles, 2016). In addition to this, RCTs are liable to influence by confounding variables such as therapist allegiance, differential attrition of participants between groups, and non-representative sampling (Carey & Stiles, 2016). In terms of practicalities, offering CGT in clinical work requires the clinician to be familiar with both IPT and CBT techniques, methods, and processes – expertise that not all clinicians are likely to have. Given this, we propose a novel CBT-based approach to working with grief in clinical settings that is based solely on the CBT model, without excluding interpersonal and socio-occupational factors that affect the grieving individual.

CBT is a well-evidenced and robust form of therapeutic intervention that is widely used in the UK; it is one of the most commonly recommended interventions for mental health difficulties by the National Institute for Health and Care Excellence (NICE). Given that CBT has a strong evidence base and is a manualised form of treatment that is widely employed, we propose a novel theoretical and clinical framework based on CBT, which can be used when working with individuals experiencing complicated grief. We suggest that the client's current difficulties are formulated within the

CBT framework using both longitudinal and cross-sectional formulation methods. We further highlight the importance of including information about the individual's memories of loss and their processing of loss (including thinking styles, attributional biases, coping styles, personality traits, mastery/control, memory, cultural/social norms, and spiritual factors).

CBT is an approach that addresses the affective and cognitive disturbances that occur in response to loss, and can help with experiences of hopelessness and sadness, as well as improving individuals' problem-solving strategies. This alone can be partially effective when working with complicated grief; however, the consideration of values, functionality, and metacognitive processes is crucial in addressing the deeper causal factors that link loss and complicated grief responses. Our novel approach integrates modern third-wave CBT approaches with an evolutionary perspective to develop a holistic theoretical and therapeutic approach to grief.

Henceforth, we use the term "complicated grief" to refer to all individuals experiencing grief that is negatively impacting their socio-occupational functioning and emotional wellbeing – this does not necessitate a formal diagnosis, but is used as shorthand for ease of communication. Additionally, we feel that focusing solely on mortality-based loss reduces this experience to one dimension, when in reality it is important to consider other facets of loss such as the loss of a relationship, a job, or a role. We use the term "the lost object", referring to the internal representation of that which is lost; this allows us to consider loss in its broadest sense (person, relationship, job, role, etc.) and hence to approach loss in a holistic and values-based manner, as opposed to the symptom-based bereavement-oriented perspectives that dominate pre-existing models of grief.

The Principles of Loss Model

Thus far, interventions relating to loss and grief have largely been passive – a process of waiting for time to pass during which individuals move through stages, phases, or meaning-making shifts. Although recent CBT approaches have attempted to address this, they do not fully encompass the active and proactive approach that our model proposes. This is because existing CBT-based models are based on the idea of "readiness" – that the client must be "ready" to process their grief, and hence use motivational interviewing (e.g. Rollnick et al., 2010) techniques to prepare the individual for this processing. These techniques often focus on cognitive interventions such as creating pro/con lists, and focus on "resistance to therapy". However, these ways of understanding grief work foreground cognitive processes and as such enable individuals in remaining detached from the emotions, values, and function of their grief. Our approach highlights the role of primary emotions which act as barriers to actively processing loss, and ensures that emotions, cognitions, and feelings are processed simultaneously to actively navigate the impact and aftermath of loss. We suggest that starting with one of these three areas of experience, as opposed to all three, is limiting as it stagnates the therapy and prevents individuals from confronting their pain.

In order to achieve this, we propose the Principles of Loss. This model encompasses metacognition, values, and compassion to provide a comprehensive and active intervention for loss. The remainder of this chapter focuses on supporting individuals to face the possibility of engaging with the changes that have occurred as a result of loss, which in turn enables them to talk about and process the loss itself in an active manner. This approach is characterised by scaffolding individuals to talk about the loss and its meaning in relation to core values, explore the emotional impact, and how the loss has affected their day-to-day functioning.

Subsequent chapters provide guidance on assessment, formulation, case conceptualisation, treatment planning, and supervision. The Principles of Loss model is further couched within an understanding of evolutionary processes, cultural diversities, and individual differences, allowing this approach to be tailored to the needs of each client based on their social, cultural, and lived experiences.

The Evolutionary Perspective

Emotions and Their Roles

There is much debate within the field of psychology relating to the primacy of cognitions versus emotions. The following overview is based on Hashempour (2016), which outlines the cognition and emotion debate in relation to measuring and predicting psychological wellbeing. In the face of a triggering event or context, researchers have debated whether the emotion is elicited first (Zajonc, 1984), or if the cognition precedes the emotion (Lazarus, 1984). This is an important distinction, as it influences the theoretical and clinical approach to be taken. If emotions are primary, we would focus our energies on emotional regulation in order to improve a person's experience of threats. Conversely, if cognitions are primary, the focus would be on cognitive restructuring to change the meaning of the stressor and hence the experience of that trigger.

Cognitions can be defined as the mental processes by which information is perceived, processed, and evaluated in order to produce a response (Power & Dalgleish, 1999). Here, we define emotions as "energy in motion" (Watkins, 2015); automatic physiological responses to stimuli. We differentiate this from "feelings" which are the end-product of a process by which the individual notices their emotional (physiological) response, and cognitively appraises it in order to create an idiosyncratic meaning which is labelled as a feeling for example I'm standing in front of a crowd to give a speech. I notice tension in my shoulders and butterflies in my stomach; I interpret this to mean that I'm feeling anxious and scared. In this example, the physical experience is the emotion (tension, butterflies in the stomach), and the emotion is the outcome of the cognitive processing (therefore I must be anxious).

In reshaping the way emotions are considered within the therapeutic space, we can align both with the work of Lazarus and that of Zajonc; from our perspective, these positions are not mutually exclusive – it is merely a lack of mechanistic theory which has positioned them as opposites thus far. Here, we propose a mechanism of action that ties together the primacy of emotion and the primacy of cognition. We suggest that emotions are essentially electrical impulses in the brain and body that can be triggered externally (e.g. physical contexts and events) and internally (e.g. imagination, memory, etc.). When an emotion is triggered by a stimulus, there are two possible pathways of action: (1) the emotion (physiological sensation) is cognitively appraised and interpreted; meaning is ascribed to the emotion in the form of a feeling, or (2) the emotion may move directly into feeling, based on prior experiences and familiarity with the emotion and its idiosyncratic meanings. Cognitive appraisals can be negative or positive, and these interpretations are learned/automated over time to produce the second action pathway described earlier.

In accordance with Lazarus and Folkman (1987), we apply the transactional model of stress here. This model suggests that cognitive processing occurs in two stages: primary and secondary appraisal. Primary appraisals relate to the individual's thinking, attributional, and attentional styles which are developed through a confluence of inherited temperament and lived experiences. Secondary appraisals relate to the ways in which the individual is able to cope with the outcome of the primary appraisal. These are coping strategies the individual has developed over time to navigate internal and external triggers. This is essentially the management of experience; how a person copes with their internal responses to internal and external stimuli.

Furthermore, we include here the adaptive information processing model by Shapiro and Laliotis (2011). This model describes that information is stored at 2 levels: memory and body. Sometimes in the absence of cognitive components, the body still notices the threat and responds accordingly. The same is true vice versa: threat can be triggered through memory recall (intrusions/flashbacks) in the absence of body sensations. This has been built on by trauma theorists who have shown that information is stored in different ways in the brain and body, and how this influences here-and-now experiences. Hartman and Burgess (1993) describe how lived experiences are processed and stored in relation to sensory, perceptual, cognitive, and interpersonal information. Memory encoding, retrieval, and recall are similarly affected by these factors, and in turn influence future experiences. In the context of trauma or traumatic loss, experiences may be processed in a fragmented or impartial manner due to the overwhelming nature of internal and external stimuli, leading to the formation of disjointed, highly emotive, and distressing memories (Brewin & Holmes, 2003). These memories behave differently to non-traumatic autobiographical memories: trauma memories tend to be recalled involuntarily (e.g. flashbacks, nightmares), have overgeneralised triggers, and conscious recall is fragmented – preventing thorough processing of experiences and hence inhibiting the reprocessing of trauma memories into a non-trauma memory format (i.e. which is characterised by conscious and voluntary recall, contextualisation to time and place, and longitudinal flow of time). Neuropsychological studies have found evidence for these qualitative differences between trauma and non-trauma autobiographical memories, suggesting physical differences in their modes of processing, encoding, retrieval, and recall (Bourne et al., 2013).

Within the context of loss, emotions are being constantly triggered both internally and externally, which are appraised as threats, and hence the feeling is a response to these emotions and cognitions may present as a state of shock. We develop specific strategies to cope with external and internal triggers – flipping from threat to the safety and back again throughout our lives. This process may be heightened in intensity or frequency of oscillation in the aftermath of loss. When someone is highly distressed, they may be unable to figure out a coping strategy for such an overwhelming amount of emotive stimulation. Therefore, the simplest way to cope is to stay there – frozen, in shock – until the threat has passed. The individual's best chance of survival may be to "wait out the storm" – to remain cocooned within a state of freeze until they feel able to actively do something to cope with the experience of the loss itself. Psychotherapeutic intervention in this instance therefore focuses on enabling the person to manage their experiences more efficiently.

Threat and Protection

The human brain and body have evolved over millennia to ensure the survival of the species (Darwin, 1859). Adaptations that have a threat-detection function have been vital in ensuring the success of the human race; the importance of detecting threats from external (e.g. predators) and internal (e.g. pain) signals has been widely documented in the extant literature (e.g. Nesse, 1994; Stein & Nesse, 2011) as well as the neurobiological mechanisms by which these threat systems function to keep us safe (Woody & Szechtman, 2011). The role of the threat system in cognitive-affective processing (Stein & Nesse, 2011) as well as implications for psychological wellbeing are central to the compassion-focused therapy (CFT; Gilbert, 2010) approach. This model of mental health highlights the importance of focusing on innate systems that regulate hormonal, appetitive, sensory, behavioural, cognitive, and affective information processing and output under conditions of threat.

According to social mentality theory (Gilbert, 2014, 2016), humans first developed the system for relating to others, and this system was then utilised for individuals to be able to relate to themselves. Here we see the importance of community and relatedness, and how this forms the basis for self-to-self processing. Social relating systems are based on patterns of cognitions, emotions, feelings, and behaviours in relation to social challenges to survive – such as competition, cooperation, and care-seeking (Hermanto & Zuroff, 2016). Social mentalities orient individuals to social roles and rules, which guide how others' behaviours are interpreted, and determine how a person responds in a given situation. These processes are enabled by the human capacity for imagination, self-reflection, and self-awareness (Hermanto & Zuroff, 2016). Social mentalities can be activated in the presence of others and also when alone – for example through imagination. Social mentality theory (Gilbert, 2014, 2016) suggests that these ways of self–other and self–self relating have evolved over time to increase chances of adaptation and survival – hence are protective mechanisms for human beings.

Threat-based models are vital to our understanding of brain–body–environment interactions, and are well-evidenced in their centrality to human experience, adaptation, and survival (Boyer & Bergstrom, 2011). However, what these approaches neglect is the protective element of evolutionary mechanisms. There is a duality to the adaptive safety mechanisms; they both seek to detect and move away from threat, and to detect and move towards protection. Hence the threat and protective systems can be conceptualised as two sides of the same coin; in behavioural terms, both aversive conditioning and satiating conditioning are required to produce meaningful and long-lasting behavioural and affective changes (Skinner, 1965). In addition to the duality of the threat/protection system is a communicative element: displaying the perceived threat or protection in a socially meaningful manner serves as a signal to others in one's social network to either move away from the threat or towards the protection. Such communication also signals to others that one is in need of help or support – which serves the function of strengthening interpersonal bonds, and providing both parties with reciprocal roles that fulfil their emotional and physical needs (e.g. supporter – supported; Brown, 2018).

Additionally, the body has many ways in which to ensure its own safety, evolved over time to maximise survival. One such mechanism which may become activated in the context of loss is the "freeze" response (Barrett, 2012). Here, we refer not only to a physical state of freeze whereby the individual experiences an inability to move, but also an emotional state of freeze (Feeny et al., 2000) – numbness and emotional distancing – as a form of protection against psychological and emotional threat. Following loss, an individual may experience a prolonged state of emotional freeze – feeling "frozen in time" which can be conceptualised as a protective (and likely unconscious) coping strategy that serves to prevent the individual from directly experiencing the pain of the loss until they feel able to cope. Therefore, the length of time that this emotional freeze occurs cannot be estimated; it varies greatly depending on the individual's temperament, previous losses and coping styles, and the current context in which they are grieving.

Cognitive empathy (perspective taking) and emotional empathy are evolutionarily ancient (Smith, 2006) and have developed over millennia in humans to serve a protective function in the form of social altruism (De Waal, 2008). Empathy-based altruism provides a protective mechanism by which survival is enhanced and is intrinsically rewarding at the individual level. This demonstrates the importance of considering protective processes in the context of loss and grief; building on an individual's strengths and empathic altruism. Developing deep emotional bonds with others in our social network increases the protection available to us; being able to signal to those individuals during times of distress (i.e. mourning) and to access their support is necessary for survival. Although it is a popular belief that having a social network is in itself sufficient in buffering the negative impact of loss on an individual's emotional wellbeing, this is not necessarily the case (Stroebe et al., 2005). It is the goodness of fit between the individual's needs and the ability of the social network to meet those needs that is important (Walker et al., 1977). This is understandable from an evolutionary perspective, given that the loss constitutes a significant deprivation of the individual's ability to meet their needs and hence continue to function within their socio-occupational contexts. Given this, considering not only the presence/absence of a social network, but the idiosyncratic meaning of the loss and the specific functional impairments created by the loss is necessary when working therapeutically with grief.

It is important to our survival to be able to detect threat from internal and external signals. For example, if someone is experiencing a lack of confidence, they would have a combination of both – an internally developed threat system linked to their beliefs, and external affirmation of their experiences (i.e. looking for confirmation). This becomes prominent in the way they function – becomes observable to others. For example, the individual may say "I've always been shy" – reporting that from an early age, they have been aware of the threat system. This becomes reinforced by external information over time through the confirmation bias (Oswald & Grosjean, 2004). Therefore, internal and external experiences are brought into alignment by the cognitive appraisal systems. Becoming hypervigilant to external threats as a result of noticing distressing emotions (physiological sensations) is adaptive and protective, as it can help the individual to regulate their emotions and prevent further distress. It can also become unhelpful in the long term as it leads to a confirmation of their beliefs about the self, hence reducing opportunities for alternative narratives about the self to be developed (McLean et al., 2007). These patterns of meaning-making can become automated, with emotions being short-circuited to feelings (noticing tension -> I'm shy), which can result in predictable or rigid patterns of coping. In the context of loss, such a lack of flexibility in identity and coping styles can be to the detriment of the individual, as this can prevent them from actively confronting their loss and hence reduces the possibility of processing occurring spontaneously.

Similarly, the anticipation of loss can have a protective function. Anticipatory loss can relate to loss of self or loss of others, and may be accompanied by a sense of self-pity. For example, with thoughts such as "If I / they die, I / we won't have these experiences". Whilst a fear of death is likely present in all of us at an unconscious level – and can be a focus of some interventions, such as existential therapy (van Deurzen et al., 2019) – it is usually not at the forefront of our minds in our day-to-day lives. This is perhaps due to the fact that being constantly aware of one's own or others' mortality would be intensely distressing, and hence detriment psychological and social functionality (Cozzolino et al., 2014). Some theorists suggest that this terror of death seeps from the unconscious into our drives, motivations, and behaviours in ways we are unaware of – such as through nationalism, aggression, self-esteem, and prosocial behaviours (Pyszczynski et al., 2006). Typically, thoughts about death are avoided to reduce distress (Cozzolino et al., 2014) and increase chances of survival; however, there are times where one cannot ignore death completely. This is especially true within the current context of a global pandemic: there is a clear threat, and constant fear-based information is encountered regarding one's own and others' imminent mortality. This has led to an increase in anticipatory loss, whereby individuals are increasingly attuned to the threat, and so more and more preoccupied by the threat in their daily lives. In such instances, cognitive (e.g. worry) and behavioural coping strategies (e.g. excessive hand washing, complete social isolation) are deployed to reduce the sense of threat and increase perceived safety. Currently, such coping styles are further reinforced by government guidelines relating to COVID-19 – hence perpetuating the perceived usefulness of these strategies and alongside this, perpetuating heightened anticipatory loss and death anxiety.

Shame and Pride

There is an additional evolutionary component that must be considered when discussing loss and grief. Humans are social beings and have developed emotional responses such as pride and shame in order to help individuals discern the right and wrong way to respond in situations. These emotions act as an internal moral compass that guides people's responses in their day-to-day lives based on societal norms and rules. Shame is a powerful affective response that has significant power over people's behaviours in social contexts; the evolutionary drive to be accepted within one's community (due to its protective function) is so strong as to shape the nature of relationships and affect the individual's physiological and psychological responses (Gilbert, 2007). If an individual who has experienced a loss has a shame response, this will influence their processing of the loss, and hence negatively impact their grief. It may prolong the bereavement process, and result in a complicated grief response.

Pride has two variants: authentic pride – which is associated with self-esteem and positive psychological and social outcomes, and hubristic pride – which is associated with narcissism and negative outcomes (Tracy et al., 2020). Here we focus on authentic pride in relation to loss: if an individual who has experienced a loss responds with feelings of authentic pride (i.e. they are able to take pride in the positive relationship they had with the lost object), they will have a positive orientation to the loss, and hence be better able to process the loss in order to restore functionality in their life.

In this way, shame and authentic pride can be seen as two sides of the same coin; similarly to the threat/protection relationship outlined earlier, the valence of an individual's emotional response in the aftermath of loss (i.e. shame vs pride) has a significant impact on how they relate to that loss and hence how they process it in the long term.

Shock and Self-Blame

At times, an individual may experience shock in response to the loss, hence fail to understand how to respond appropriately. Shock can be conceptualised as a psychological startle response (Lang et al., 1990) the startle reflex is most strongly elicited for aversive stimuli; What greater aversive stimulus exists than the loss of a highly valued object? Similarly, the initial shock of loss can be conceptualised as a psychological freeze response (Bracha, 2004; Schmidt et al., 2008) whereby the threat/protective system is flooded, to the point that the individual is incapable of responding appropriately. Taken together, we can see that a startle/freeze response may be expected and appropriate in the context of loss – it functions to protect the individual's mind from the pain of the loss, and hence dampens their affective, cognitive, and behavioural responses.

In such instances, the internal norms and values are subdued by the immediate numbness caused by the loss; the individual must look to others in their social network (perhaps those with more experience – such as the elders in the community) to be led by them. The shock response and lack of understanding about how to react may later lead to thoughts such as "am I doing this right?", and "what's wrong with me?", therefore engendering a self-blaming emotional and attitudinal stance. Blame alerts the individual to the fact that they have not responded in a way that aligns with their values. This discord between an individual's values and their current emotional state can lead to further distress, hence complicating and prolonging the grief response.

Disgust

Disgust is another core emotion with an innate and evolutionarily adaptive function similar to fear, anger, and shame (Veale et al., 2015). Disgust plays an important role in noticing, attending to, and avoiding threats to the self, and can lead to the same range of responses as other core emotions that is fight, flight, freeze, submit.

Loss within the Relational Context

Unavailability

In the context of bereavement, these evolutionary principles shed new light on the function and process of grieving. The people in our social networks can be conceptualised as serving protective functions; we gravitate naturally towards those individuals who help us to feel safe and connected, who nourish our emotional needs, and provide us with a foundation from which to explore ourselves and the world. This is not a novel concept; attachment theory has a long tradition of linking innate emotional and physical needs to caregiving, and the impact of these bonds on later adult functioning (Ainsworth et al., 2015; Fonagy, 2001). Infants who are separated from their primary caregiver display a freeze response, and may express their distress through crying, reaching, and vocalisations intended to return the caregiver to the self. When the parent does not return (e.g. when a child is given up for adoption, when the caregiver separates from the family, or passes away), we see the child regress into a position of learned helplessness (Seligman, 1972). Vocalisations and crying cease, and the child becomes emotionally unresponsive. This is a response frequently seen in children who have extended hospital stays without their caregiver(s) in childhood (e.g. Alsop-Shields & Mohay, 2001; Rutter, 1979), or children raised in institutions with infrequent and unpredictable social contact from staff (e.g. Schuengel et al., 2009; Stovall & Dozier, 1998).

Using attachment and protective social networks as the baseline, we can understand how loss creates a situation in which the bereaved individual has lost a resource – a source of (emotional) support, and hence has lost one of the "tools" for survival. In instances of death, the more proximal the deceased person is to the bereaved (e.g. a close family member, partner, child), the bigger and more valued the resource, and hence the greater the impact of the loss. On the other hand, the more distal the relationship between the deceased and the bereaved (e.g. an acquaintance, a friend of a friend, etc.), the smaller and less valued the resource, and hence the lower the impact of the loss. The heuristic validity of this is evident in everyday life: the loss of a close family member is much more painful and immediately debilitating than the loss of a friend's cousin who is practically a stranger to you. The closer someone is to you emotionally (and perhaps physically), the greater your reliance on them for emotional support – therefore when they are no longer available, the greater the impact on your emotional state and your ability to function in day-to-day life.

It is, therefore, the unavailability of a valued and much-needed resource that causes such a huge functional impairment following loss. We would go so far as to suggest that the psychological community needs to re-conceptualise loss in terms of unavailability – and hence consider the impact of loss on the individual's functioning in a holistic and idiosyncratic manner.

Relying on an understanding of loss and grief that focuses only on stage- or phase-based trajectories that hinge on threat detection is too simplistic. Given more recent advancements in our theoretical and practical understanding of the human psyche, our approaches to grief need also to be updated. In the face of loss, there are two major responses exhibited: (1) a freeze response (Sagliano et al., 2014) that results in learned helplessness (Abramson et al., 1978) and chronic low mood, and (2) a complex trauma response (Williams, 2006) that is characterised by intrusions, nightmares, and rumination akin to a post-traumatic stress response.

Grief responses are idiosyncratic; the role of the clinician is to work with the individual to understand the intrinsic value the loss had for them, and the emotional needs the lost object fulfilled. In doing so, the clinician can build an understanding of the *functional* impairment created by the unavailability of the lost object, rather than focusing purely on symptom management.

Functional Impairment

The functional impairment that occurs following loss can be conceptualised using Knipe's bio-psycho-social model (Knipe, 2009). Knipe outlines five major evolutionarily adaptive systems that have developed in order to contribute to the survival (and flourishing) of the human species. They are as follows: (1) defence system (DS): fight or flight responses associated with ancient neural networks in the brainstem and cerebellum; (2) social ranking system (SRS): associated with the middle brain structures, such as the limbic system; (3) attachment system (AS): also associated with the limbic system; (4) pleasure seeking system (PSS); and (5) sexual system (SS). The function of each of these systems is to increase the organism's chances of survival; they are therefore innate in all humans.

When faced with a threat, the DS becomes activated, and functions to remove the individual from the immediate danger through the fight, flight, freeze, submit, feign death response. This is an ancient strategy that matches the current contextual threat with the individual's survival needs. The SRS is associated with social behaviours such as dominance, cooperation, pleasing others, and submission. It too is an ancient brain function that is associated with increasing an individual's chances of survival by enhancing group cohesion. When the AS is activated, we see behaviours such as proximity seeking, interpersonal avoidance, and emotional suppression. Again, this is highly adaptive in evolutionary terms as one's caregivers/social networks are the greatest strength in the face of danger for humans – who have evolved in such a way as to reduce the individual's physical abilities (e.g. we do not have claws or fangs or toughened skin) for the sake of "strength by numbers" and our higher cognitive capacities (e.g. planning, working together, etc.). The SS can be over- (hypersexuality) or under-stimulated (hyposexuality), which is also adaptive given the context; for example, in times of famine it is better to have fewer mouths to feed whereas in times of abundance, successful breeding adds to the strength of the group.

Knipe's model is typically used in the context of childhood trauma and experiences of shame; we apply it here to loss and grief. Humans are social mammals, with huge value attributed to social roles, social support/ networks, and social status. In cases of death, it is unsurprising that the loss of a valued person has an impact on these five bio-psycho-social systems, and hence on the individual's level of functioning. In the context of loss, hyperactivation of the DS results in a trauma-like fight/flight response, whereas hypoactivation of the DS results in a depressive-learned help-lessness response (which can be linked with the "feigned death" and "freeze" elements of the DS's functions). The AS is also affected by loss; the closer the relationship between the deceased and the bereaved, the greater the impact on the AS, and hence the greater the associated functional impairment. For example, when one loses a parent, there is an immediate loss of the "secure base", which can result either in hyperarousal states (e.g. psychological proximity seeking towards the deceased in the form of rumination) or hypoarousal states (e.g. suppressing or pushing away any painful thoughts about the deceased, and exercising emotional avoidance by keeping oneself busy/occupied in the present). The experiences of fear and avoidance are discussed in further detail in later sections relating to coping and compromise with the loss. The SRS is also affected by loss: depending on the role that the deceased played in the bereaved person's life, the bereaved may become more dominant in their social behaviours (e.g. increased aggression and authoritarian responses) or may become more submissive (e.g. increased passivity, allowing others to make all the decisions). If the deceased and the bereaved had a sexual relationship, the loss may result in either hyper- or hypo-sexuality as the bereaved attempts to make sense of their loss in relation to their own sexuality and sexual needs. We posit that in some individuals the PSS becomes inhibited or suppressed in times of grief; the bereaved is less inclined to seek pleasure, and also less able to experience pleasurable feelings. In others, the PSS may be overstimulated, resulting in heightened impulsivity and risk-taking behaviours as the individual fights to overcome their "numbness".

It is apparent that the functional impairments associated with each of these systems interact with one-another and compound the bereaved individual's distress. This interaction explains the earlier distinction we make between the learned helplessness-depressive response and the trauma-based response to loss. For example, the initial freeze response (DS) may be worsened by interpersonal avoidance and proximity seeking towards the deceased (AS), a submissive interpersonal style (SRS), hyposexuality (SS), and anhedonia (PSS). This results in a complex and deep-rooted learned helplessness/depressive response that prevents the individual from performing the socio-occupational and emotional functions that may be expected or required of them in their day-to-day life. On the other hand – and yet equally debilitating – is the trauma-based response: increased fight/flight responses (DS) are compounded by emotional suppression (AS), a submissive interpersonal style (SRS), hyposexuality (SS), and heightened risk-taking (PSS). The exact patterns of hypo- and hyper-stimulation of the five functional systems will vary based on the individual's temperament, personal history, relationship to the deceased, coping styles, and the context of the loss. Therefore an idiosyncratic case conceptualisation is necessary for meaningful clinical intervention to be provided.

Individual and Collective Loss

All of us exist within social systems, and correspondingly have both an individual identity and a collective identity. At times the needs, values, and goals of these identities may be complementary, and at other times be dissonant. Belonging to a collective comes with a sense of responsibility and social needs which can be met through relational experiences. Each of us, due to the multifaceted and intersecting nature of our experiences and identities, belongs to multiple social groups at any given time. For example, a person may be a woman, Black, a chemical engineer, an artist, and queer. In theory, they would hold affiliations to each of those corresponding social collectives, as well as various intersections. This individual's involvement and engagement with different elements of their own identity and different social contexts is likely to vary over time, based on other life contexts, and on the relational contexts within each group. In terms of loss, our affiliations to various social groups can act as bridges between others and ourselves, and hence widen the impact of loss to encompass the social group as a whole. A clear recent example of this is the murder of George Floyd; his death as a Black American man brutalised by the police was shared by many other Black people – both in America and all around the world, especially in White-majority countries where racism and police violence against Black bodies is rife. George Floyd's death undoubtedly created a huge impact on his immediate family, friends, and social network. Additionally, his death had a phenomenal impact on all other people who had shared identities and lived experiences with him – in this case, the Black community across the globe. Therefore, there was both individual loss (e.g. for his family) as well as collective loss (e.g. other Black people in America).

Whilst this is an example of a high-profile death that was broadcast to the world and catalysed huge social awareness, the same pattern of individual and collective loss occurs all the time. When a person is lost, there is both an individual and a collective impact on the social network. There are invisible links between people who may not personally know each other; the impact that someone's absence has can be significant even if indirect – because it taps into prior losses or values for each person who is affected. We can look to mirror neurons (Kilner & Lemon, 2013) for a neuropsychological explanation of this elicitation of collective loss. Jenee Johnson (Johnson, 2022) speaks about the activation of mirror neurons when we witness others' distress, and how this activates our own emotional systems to respond with empathy. How we value the loss is not necessarily based on the closeness – it is based on the function of that relationship.

For example, if I listen to the same music every day when I drive to work, then the loss of that artist would be painful and brought into my consciousness each day like an intrusion on the way to work. I may then experience other emotions of apprehension each morning, as I am primed to have that negative experience each day. Another example is that of losing a colleague or peer in a social club. There is a sense of individual loss, where each member of that social network grieves the loss of that person. Additionally, there is a collective loss, where the group as a whole grieves the person. This grieving process may be further complicated by the socio-functional impact of the loss. For instance, if that person held a crucial role within the team, their loss may mean that certain responsibilities need to be redistributed and roles revised. This has both a practical and emotional impact on the collective, as both individuals and the group as a whole may make different meanings of this rearrangement in their ways of working. Some may welcome a focus on the practical as a way to distance themselves psychologically from the pain of the loss. Conversely, others may resent a shift to the practicalities, as they may feel this is respectful of the person who has been lost.

Tri-Theme Model

We suggest that not all losses are negative in nature and that not all loss is characterised by grief. Loss is a marker for change: change can be positive or negative – when the change is positive, it is accompanied by feelings of relief and elation; where change is negative, emotions such as pain, sadness, shame, and blame arise. A negative response to loss occurs when there is a conflict between the loss and one's values. We consider grief to be the cognitive and emotional disturbances that occur in the aftermath of loss, and bereavement to be the process of coming to terms with the loss. Whether a person perceives the loss to be positive or negative, and whether or not they experience a grieving process, is dependent on their values. Although loss and grief are universal, the mourning behaviours (e.g. rituals, customs) vary across cultures as they are socially constructed, as do the specific values that individuals hold – these are determined by the norms and rules of their socio-cultural context.

Our approach is embedded in evolutionary psychology and draws on the theoretical and therapeutic frameworks of third-wave CBT approaches such as CFT (Gilbert, 2010) and acceptance and commitment therapy (ACT; Hayes et al., 2009). We have integrated these approaches as they are grounded in a values-based perspective that focuses on the protective mechanisms available to individuals during times of hardship. The reason that our approach focuses heavily on third-wave CBT approaches is due to their grounding in a values-driven formulation of emotional distress that foregrounds functionality rather than symptomatology.

This novel conceptualisation of grief is based on the two major responses to loss outlined above: learned helplessness and complex trauma. We posit that these are not mutually exclusive states of being and that individuals may shift from one to the other and back again countless times during the processing of their grief. The focus is not on symptomatology, but on functionality; as clinicians, we must continually assess and reassess the impact of the loss on the bereaved individual in terms of their daily emotional, physical, and socio-occupational functioning in order to understand the idiosyncratic grieving process as it unfolds. It is important to note that grieving is a *process*, and as such there is no fixed trajectory or linearity to it; grief is complex and dynamic, hence we must be prepared to continually assess and formulate an individual's functional impairments following loss in order to help them move towards a more functional way of being.

Below is our simplified model for the treatment of grief (Figure 1.1); it will be explained and expanded upon in further detail in Chapters 2 and 3. This is an overarching framework within which clinicians can work with individuals exhibiting learned helplessness- and/or trauma-based responses to the loss. The primary presentation of learned helplessness/trauma can be addressed using existing approaches as recommended by the NICE in order to allow the individual to stabilise their mood, prior to beginning grief work. For learned helplessness-related chronic depression, we recommend the use of a Beckian approach involving behavioural activation, pleasure-/mastery-based activity scheduling, and cognitive restructuring (Beck, 2979). For trauma-based presentations, we recommend the use

Simplified Treatment Pathway

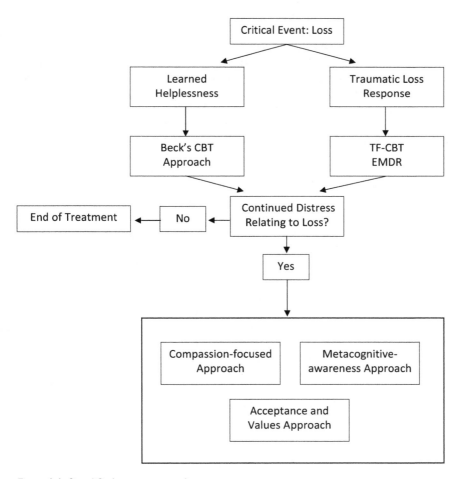

Figure 1.1 Simplified treatment pathway.

of the trauma-focused CBT approach (Ehlers & Clark, 2000) or Eye Movement Desensitisation and Reprocessing (EMDR; Shapiro, 2017).

Following this initial stabilisation phase, grief work can commence. This stabilisation is necessary as without it, the individual is likely to be too distressed, or too "stuck" to engage with the challenges of grief work. Once the individual has attained a sense of stability and their motivation to engage with their loss has increased, we can begin the grief work. Imagine experiencing two types of pain: one is a sharp external pain whereas the other is a dull internal pain. The sharpness and immediacy of the external pain masks and obscures the dull internal pain; the external pain cannot be ignored, or it will impede any progress towards the internal pain. Therefore, we can use traditional CBT/trauma-focused approaches to manage the sharp external pain prior to addressing the deeper emotional pain of the loss itself. If, following the stabilisation treatment, the individual becomes "unstuck" and is able to process their grief independently, grief work is not necessary – and may in fact be contraindicated (Hall, 2014). This novel grief treatment approach is designed for those individuals experiencing "complex grief", whose functional impairment is not alleviated following the CBT/trauma-focused work and who continue to experience significant distress relating to the loss *in spite of* completing the stabilisation phase of treatment.

We propose a trifold approach encompassing increasing the individual's self-compassion, self-awareness, and acceptance. Increasing compassion towards the self enables the individual to cope better with their current situation – they will be better able to tolerate their distress and to reframe it as a natural and understandable response to a challenging situation. Increasing the bereaved individual's awareness of the impact of the loss for them personally – the functional impact – helps them to become aware of what has changed and how, and hence cope in a more helpful way with the loss. Finally, bringing an element of acceptance to the situation allows the individual to consider the loss from a broader perspective, and to cope better by shifting their focus towards valued action and leading a meaningful life. We suggest that these three approaches are sufficient, but not all necessary, for the processing of grief. For some individuals, the compassion approach alone will be sufficient to help them become "unstuck"; for others, it will be a combination of two of the factors; for others still, it may be that all three approaches are required in order to fully reintegrate them with meaningful activities and move them in the direction of a valued life. This approach is not prescriptive; it provides an explanatory model for grief that is intended to be used flexibly and dynamically, through the use of idiosyncratic formulations that are based on functional analysis of the impact of the loss.

Outlined below are the three major components of this model. The basic theoretical basis is provided, and its links to our model of grief. We suggest that readers who are unfamiliar with the compassion-focused, metacognitive, and acceptance-based models refer to the following key readings, as it is beyond the scope of this book to provide comprehensive guidance on all three: Gilbert (2010), Schraw and Moshman (1995), and Harris (2019). As it appears in the simplified treatment pathway diagram earlier, the following three approaches can be used in any order and any combination with each bereaved individual based on their idiosyncratic case conceptualisation. We present below the compassionate approach, used in order to build resilience, followed by the metacognitive approach to help individuals process what they have lost and what that means to them, and lastly the acceptance model to help the individual make meaning from the loss, and process their grief in a way that moves them in the direction of their values.

Compassion-Focused Approach

It is common for individuals who have suffered a loss and are processing complex grief to experience heightened levels of self-criticism, self-doubt, guilt, anger, and shame. These mental states can be highly distressing, and further compound the challenges of processing the loss. High levels of anger, shame, guilt, and self-criticism are also likely to block the person from processing the sadness and pain associated with grief; they can become a form of subtle cognitive and affective avoidance that prevents the individual from meaningfully connecting with their experiences of the loss itself. It is important, therefore, to guide bereaved individuals towards a more compassionate frame of mind, through which lens they are able to view themselves, the world, and the future. This shift in perspective allows individuals to let in the painful experiences associated with loss, to tolerate and "sit with" such mental states, and to hold an attitude of compassion towards the self which builds strength and resilience in the face of loss.

The compassionate approach we integrate in this model is based on Paul Gilbert's formulation of psychological wellbeing (Gilbert, 2010). We augment this pre-existing approach through our focus on the protective system *as well as* the threat system, and their roles in the impact and processing of loss. Based on the evolutionary approach, the compassion model acknowledges that we are all here with our "tricky brains", and that at times we can respond to situations in ways that are not helpful – such as responses that increase our distress, and those that prevent us from processing events in a way that allows us to move forwards from them in a meaningful manner. This approach places emphasis on shifting out of the threat mode and into the soothing system; this enables individuals to activate positive and pleasurable emotions, cognitions, and behaviours that help them to feel safe – and hence make decisions based on what is important to them, rather than based on fight-or-flight responses that are based purely on survival. The compassionate approach helps individuals to build their understanding of how the mind works, and to begin exercising self-compassion. This builds resilience, and allows the individual to feel stronger when faced with life's difficulties. It is also an approach that shifts away from a blaming stance, and helps the individual to understand that whilst it is not their fault that things have turned out the way that they have, that they have the ability to take responsibility for themselves and their responses in the future.

Linking this with the evolutionary approach outlined earlier, group membership brings adaptive benefits such as social support and facilitating emotional wellbeing. People have both individual and group identities, consisting of beliefs, values, and behavioural patterns. These identities can be helpful or unhelpful in the context of loss depending on whether there is a sense of competition or collaboration. If an individual prioritises the collective over the self, they are more likely to behave in collaborative ways which reciprocally support others and the self. On the other hand, if an individual prioritises the self over the collective, they are more likely to behave in competitive ways which may be less compassionate towards others. In the context of loss, we may see this occurring when individuals either do or don't feel supported by their communities. For example, an individual whose personal belief in God has been shaken by the loss may feel at odds with their religious community and may take a more competitive stance – thereby distancing themselves from the community in order to manage their own individual wellbeing. Conversely, an individual whose belief in God has been strengthened by the loss may seek their community more and engage in collaborative behaviours to receive and provide social support during a time of distress.

In the context of our model, we would socialise bereaved individuals to this CFT model, and help them to begin the process of building self-care into their daily routine. For some individuals, it would be pertinent to explore the CFT model more fully, and to help them understand their current experience of grief in the context of their early experiences, key fears, coping strategies, and the unintended consequences of those coping strategies (CFT longitudinal formulation). For others, the self-care and self-compassion element (achieved mainly through the use of psychoeducation and imagery exercises) will be sufficient to build the resilience required to continue grief work through metacognitive- and/or acceptance-based work. As noted earlier, the number and combination of these three therapeutic elements required for each individual are not prescriptive; the approach taken will depend entirely on the case conceptualisation and formulation (explored further in Chapter 3).

Metacognitive Awareness Approach

It is well known that individuals who have experienced a significant loss are likely to use coping strategies that rely on being cognitively and emotionally avoidant; this often manifests as excessive rumination about the past and excessive worrying about the future. The person must escape into the past or the future because being in the present is (unconsciously) felt to be unbearable. Therefore, individuals oscillate between rumination and worry constantly. For example, recalling a memory of the deceased results in increased ruminative thoughts. Those ruminations may be compared with the here-and-now (in which the deceased is absent) as well as compared with the future (a future in which the deceased is no longer going to play a role). This leads to worrying about the future, a process that is maintained and enhanced by negative predictions about a future without the deceased.

We can see in this process that the bereaved is caught in a loop between the past (which is idealised) and the future (which is denigrated) – without spending much (if any) time in the present. We can infer here that they place greater value and perceive as more fulfilling those previous experiences with the deceased, in comparison to the predicted future which feels hopeless and bleak. These processes are often occurring at an unconscious level; consciously, the individual may be avoiding thinking about the loss as a way of coping with the challenges of daily life. However, unconscious processes perceive the psychic wound, and gravitate towards it until that issue is resolved. Therefore, these shifts from rumination to worry are the result of (unconscious) metacognitive processes that are bringing unresolved issues into the conscious mind in order to process them (Schraw & Moshman, 1995). However, when the conscious mind is busy trying to cope with everyday tasks, these underlying metacognitive processes have reduced power (due to excessive cognitive load). Therefore, engagement with activities in the present indirectly suppresses metacognitive processing of the loss.

We see the reverse of this when people go to bed; their cognitive capacity is freed from demanding tasks, and they often report a significant increase in rumination and worry when they are trying to fall asleep. Often, these thought patterns that oscillate between rumination and worry result in emotions such as shame, guilt, fear, and anger – which maintain the difficulty by preventing the individual from engaging meaningfully with the loss itself. Sadness and irritability may also be present, although these are likely to be masked by other affective states that are "safer" to express, such as guilt. When working with bereaved individuals, we must consider these cognitive and metacognitive processes that are creating and maintaining dysfunction in the present – which includes cognitive, affective, physiological, and behavioural responses. This self-perpetuating process is depicted in Figure 1.2.

The reflective element of the diagram refers to rumination about the past, the "potential" refers to worries about the future, and "loss" is the current threat that the person is experiencing. During the grieving process, the individual oscillates constantly between these three states, leading to a sense of despair as there is no available solution to the "problem" at hand that is there is no way to bring the lost object back. Feelings of

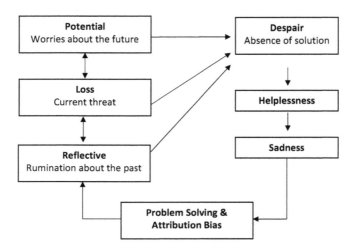

Figure 1.2 Metacognitive processes.

despair give way to helplessness and sadness, and there may also be anger – towards the self and towards the lost object. The individual may try to problem-solve their way out of the situation – a coping method that has been adaptive throughout evolution (Lazarus, 2000) – but the existence of an attentional bias that reorients the person to the loss results in a loop that feeds back into rumination and worry, and further unsuccessful problem-solving attempts. The problem-solving attempts serve to reinforce this cycle and hence prevent the individual from shifting away from oscillating between worry, rumination, and despair.

Furthermore, the brain is unable to cope with not knowing, as described by what we have named as the "bridging principle." The mind seeks certainties, which are impossible to attain in the context of loss. Individuals attempt continuously to find a resolution for the "problem" but are unable to do so. In the absence of an "answer," a loop begins whereby the mind returns to the "problem" and restarts the problem-solving process in an attempt to come to some form of resolution. This continual looping back to the "problem" is a natural and necessary process that aids survival. In times of intense distress, it may occur at an unconscious level in the form of trauma- or OCD-like intrusions. We conceptualise this as the brain's way of keeping the problem "online" and active, to try continually to solve the problem. When in distress, this is the brain's way of keeping the information active and preventing it from being lost (rumination, worry). It also may be broken down by the brain to reduce the cognitive load and make the problem-solving easier (fragmentation of memories, partial recall). The loss itself is one part of the experience, and the meaning that is made of the loss is the other part: it is the meaning-making that leads to a secondary effect – a change in feelings, beliefs, and functionality.

If the person is able to shift their attention from the problem to an alternative task or activity, it enables them to create distance between themselves and the unknown solution to the problem, hence interrupting the bridging process. However, to exit the loop entirely, the individual must process the meaning of the loss in a way that facilitates acceptance. Doing so allows the person to abandon this coping strategy (problem-solving), hence preventing the need for the bridging principle to be activated. It is the maintenance of this cycle that prevents the individual from reaching a place of acceptance; the metacognitive approach therefore helps the person to break out of the loop and hence process the loss itself.

We posit that individuals with greater problem-solving skills and higher levels of perfectionistic traits would have greater metacognitive challenges in coping with loss – and hence would be more likely to be caught in this vicious cycle. For example, if someone is "a worrier", they are likely to be constantly ruminating about the loss, attempting to solve an unsolvable problem, and hence increasing their despair, hopelessness, and sadness in the present. They may attempt to problem-solve the past (via rumination) and the future (via worry), including issues not relating to the lost object – which again reinforces the feeling of stuckness and loss, hence preventing the individual from moving towards acceptance.

Helping the individual to become aware of this vicious cycle, and to become more consciously aware of what they have lost is an important first step. In this approach, we suggest that clinicians focus on helping individuals to understand the value of the deceased, the cost of losing them, and the bereaved individual's perceptions of the future as a result of this loss. We also focus on helping the bereaved differentiate between what things were like in the past by combating the black-and-white splitting of the past as being an idealised "perfect" time and the future as a denigrated "bleak" time. This work would include addressing any splitting (black-and-white) thinking in relation to the deceased, to help the bereaved form a whole picture of the lost person, rather than a one-dimensional picture that cannot be fully processed or integrated into their autobiographical narrative.

Following this, working within our model, we encourage individuals to differentiate between what has happened in the past, and what will happen in the future, and to do this by helping them to be more present in the here-and-now. It is important to note that we focus here on the cause of symptoms (metacognitive processes) rather than the symptoms themselves (emotions, cognitions, behaviours). Basing a therapeutic approach on symptoms without addressing the core causal factors may result in the reduction of distress, but will not in the long-term alleviate the difficulty. Therefore, a metacognitive formulation of the meanings the individual attaches to the loss (Schraw, 1998), and the unconscious cause of symptoms, is a key factor to consider when working with grief.

Acceptance and Values Approach

Once the individual has built the strength, resilience, and insight required to be able to be present in the here-and-now, a values-based approach can be taken. Whilst we acknowledge that ACT is a complete treatment model in its own right, we have integrated only some elements of Harris's (2009) ACT model into our holistic approach. We suggest that the full hexaflex model is not necessary when working with grief, and instead propose the use of the triflex, as these are the key components required when working meaningfully with grief.

The ACT triflex is based on three main tenets, which relate to our conceptualisation of grief in the following manner: (1) being present in the here-and-now, as opposed to oscillating between rumination and worry; (2) accepting that the loss has occurred, and choosing to be open to the possibility of a life without the deceased; and (3) moving towards one's values in the context of the loss, by building a meaningful life that incorporates the loss and the deceased.

It is important for clinicians to understand the degree to which the bereaved has accepted their loss, which is dependent on the value that they place on the deceased – and hence the impact of that loss on their current functioning. By conceptualising the loss in terms of the protective/threat system (what function did the deceased play, and how impactful is the loss of this person?), we can ascertain the value of the loss and hence the way in which to help the bereaved process their grief.

The meaning that an individual makes of the loss has a significant impact on their emotional experience of the loss as well as their coping. The meaning-making coping model (Park, 2005) provides a clear framework for conceptualising this process. Individuals have global beliefs about the nature of the world and global goals consisting of their values and motivations. In the advent of a stressor such as loss, the individual creates appraised meanings. Appraised meanings include the nature of the stressor (e.g. loss, threat) and causal attributions (e.g. punishment, coincidence). This leads to a comparison of the global meanings and appraised meanings – where there is a discrepancy, it leads to inner conflict and emotional distress. The appraised meanings also inform the coping strategies that the individual employs to manage their distress. For example, if an individual believes in an inherently benevolent God, but their appraised meaning of loss is "I am being punished", they may experience significant inner distress – a compounded effect of the grief of the loss itself, along with inner conflict about their religious/spiritual beliefs. In order to come to resolution, the individual must either amend their appraised belief (e.g. "this is a test that I can overcome") or they must change their global beliefs (e.g. "God is punitive, and I do not want to believe in a God who can cause such suffering"). If there is no discrepancy between appraised and global meanings, the individual is able to cope with the stressor and continue functioning in their day-to-day life without experiencing this level of internal turmoil.

In the context of loss and the ACT triflex, global meanings contain an individual's core values. Accessing these during assessment and treatment helps both clinicians and clients to explore how the loss is being made sense of, and how this meaning-making is impacting the person's emotional and social functioning. Exploring the reasons for a person's distress following loss can help elucidate points of discrepancy in meaning-making, and hence provide pathways for treatment.

Socio-Cultural Awareness

Introduction

There are many factors relating to socio-cultural contexts which are important to consider when working therapeutically. As it is beyond the scope of this book to explore each area of identity in depth, we refer readers to Burnham's social GGRRAAACCEEESSS (Burnham, 2018) covering the following: gender, geography, race, religion, age, ability, appearance, class, culture, ethnicity, education, employment, sexuality, sexual orientation, and spirituality. We refer readers to Beck (2016) and Hays (2008) who provide comprehensive guidance on culturally competent clinical practice in CBT.

The focus of this section is to outline some areas of socio-cultural experience and identity which may influence the ways in which individuals process and cope with loss. We hope to highlight elements of identity which may be less visible or spoken about (Burnham, 2018). Reflecting on identity and how the intersectional experiences of both client and therapist interact in the therapeutic space is vital for providing high-quality care. Developing reflexivity as a skill is especially important when the clinician positions themselves as being culturally distant (Hashempour, 2008) from the client. Cultural distance refers to the position that we take (the distance we create) between ourselves as clinicians and the client. We develop this way of processing information about others through our socialisation and systematic categorisation of self and others into social groups. This may become especially apparent in supervision in the language clinicians use to describe clients, and the elements of clients' identities that are salient in clinicians' minds and hence are brought for discussion. The unconscious prioritisation of some elements of identity over others in clinicians' minds is often unexamined both in therapeutic and supervisory contexts. Awareness of this process and its impact on how we position ourselves in relation to clients is a key reflexive and reflective activity that clinicians need to engage in.

Reflecting on the cultural distance that we create and enact in therapeutic work allows us to examine how we view clients, and which areas of their identity we may unconsciously be prioritising or de-prioritising based on our own intersectional experiences. When perceived social distance is great, the threat system is more likely to be activated – hence creating a greater imbalance between cognition and emotion for the therapist. This decreases the likelihood of an attuned and empathic stance, hence may disrupt the therapeutic relationship. The clinician needs to be able to reflect on their own positioning and remain neutral in order to provide empathic therapy. All individuals grapple with the balance of life – the need to maintain a balance between cognition and emotion in order to maintain the "axis of self" – a centred identity that provides a sense of stability. When clients experiencing loss access therapy, their axis of self is likely to be inaccessible to them; they may be too overwhelmed with emotion, or too immersed in cognitive processing to be able to achieve the balance of life. Therapists provide an anchoring point in the client's journey to recovery – therefore the clinician needs to maintain their axis of self in order to provide this for clients.

We find the incorporation of actual identity and virtual identity (Goffman, 1959) to be useful here. Goffman differentiated between how an individual experiences themselves in contrast to how they present themselves to others. He suggested that we portray ourselves in a particular way to others, but internally have a different identity. As the distance between actual and virtual identities increases, so too does distress. We suggest that in the aftermath of loss, the distance between real and virtual identities may increase, and serve to perpetuate and magnify an individual's distress. An individual's virtual self may change following loss, perhaps leading others to comment "you're not like yourself anymore" – this may be due to a change in the actual self which, beset by guilt or shame, is now characterised by "I hate myself". As in this example, changes in the actual self may be displayed in the virtual self.

Culture plays a great role in this process of navigating the actual and virtual selves. For some, their relational, familial, community, and social contexts may be supporting and nurturing. This may help them to decrease the distance between the actual and virtual self, thereby expressing their pain in a safe environment in order to get their emotional needs met. On the other hand, if the context is one of invalidation or minimisation, the individual may feel a need to present a virtual identity that is significantly different from the actual identity. For example, an individual may feel social pressure to present themselves as "having it together", remaining "calm" and performing their duties without being outwardly distressed. This may be in huge contrast to their actual identity, where shame, fear, guilt, and sadness may be overwhelming their ability to cope. The greater the contextual pressures to perform a certain type of virtual self, the greater the likelihood of discrepancy with the actual self, and hence the greater the distress.

It is possible to link the work of Goffman (1959) to acculturation (Berry, 2003). Acculturation is a process by which an individual adjusts and adapts to the culture around them. The degree to which acculturation is necessary depends on various factors, such as the extent to which the individual's culture of origin differs from their current contextual culture, and the perceived societal pressures to "fit in" (Berry, 2003). Acculturation is not itself inherently "good" or "bad'; it arises as a consequence of social differences, and individuals may acculturate to different extents based on the need to do so. Considering this from an evolutionary perspective, it may in certain times and contexts be *necessary* for an individual to acculturate – to assimilate with the culture that surrounds them – to ensure their survival. For example, a forced migrant may be required to learn the language and customs of the country they have newly entered in order to earn a living. In this case, acculturating to a certain degree has positive impact on the individual's wellbeing and quality of life. In other instances, acculturation may not be useful. For example, an individual who has experienced war and multiple losses as a result of warfare may seek refuge in a neighbouring country whose leaders and people have not acted to support the oppressed peoples in their country of origin. They may therefore feel anger towards the culture of their new place of residence and resent the cultural forces acting to acculturate them. Furthermore, the process of acculturation is incredibly nuanced, especially when we take into account sub-cultures and other contextual influences which may determine an individual's social environment.

The degree to which an individual has acculturated (segregation, integration, assimilation, marginalisation) influences the virtual self that they are able to present in the face of loss, and hence their level of distress and the coping strategies they use to manage this distress. If an individual's culture of origin teaches certain values and beliefs in relation to loss which are at odds with that of their current contextual culture, they may experience a significant discrepancy between the actual and virtual identities, hence exacerbating their distress in relation to the loss. As clinicians, we need to be attuned to these intricacies of culture and selfhood in order to unpick where an individual's distress may be stemming from, the ways in which this distress impacts their functioning.

We posit that clinicians need to develop their reflexive skills in order to provide empathic, attuned, and useful therapy for clients. Furthermore, we believe that the application of our model enables comprehensive consideration of diverse identities and lived experiences; this approach is grounded in idiosyncratic meaning-making and formulation which focuses strongly on the relational and contextual factors that influence an individual's experience of loss, coping, and functionality. Careful consideration of diverse lived experiences is not an adjunct to our approach, but intrinsic to it. Whilst we acknowledge that clinicians must "do the work" to unlearn socialised biases and prejudices which underpin systems of power and privilege, we do not seek to explore this in detail here. Instead, we provide a brief overview of specific areas of identity which may significantly impact the grieving process. We also include a section dedicated to outlining grief responses in the context of natural disaster – namely, the coronavirus pandemic that has devastated the world in recent years.

Grief and Intersectional Identities

The aim of this section is to explore some areas of diverse experience which may influence the processes and mechanics of loss and grief. We suggest that some aspects of the experience of loss and grief are shared across socio-cultural groups, whereas others differ in terms of customs, rituals, displays of emotion, and the impact of loss on an individual's social relationships and functioning. To better understand this, we frame loss within an evolutionary framework – re-labelling loss as "change". This means that loss is equated with change in one's life – whether that be change in functionality, relationships, ability to manage, or other important areas of living that are affected by the loss. Interestingly, we all constantly experience changes in life – yet the key difference with loss-as-change is that this type of change has the potential to constantly draw one's attention to the change in an attempt to find a resolution – to un-change the change.

The ways in which individuals display, process, and overcome loss-as-change differs across cultures. There is a vast literature on the differences in expressions of grief across communities – from those who mourn in silence, to those who lament loudly. Similarly, there are socio-cultural differences in the norms associated with processing loss; the amount of time that is deemed socially acceptable for mourning and grief varies across groups, as well as the expectations of the individual who is grieving. For instance, some cultures may expect the bereaved to "move on" and continue functioning in society without outward signs of showing their suffering, whereas others may expect individuals to display their grief and permit those individuals to step back from their usual roles and responsibilities in this period of time.

Taking an evolutionary perspective, we believe that socio-cultural groups exist to facilitate survival by providing support, community, and unity. Belongingness and inclusion in social groups create a sense of safety, beings meaning to life, and can enable individuals to cope with life stressors through the provision of emotional and practical support. Membership within social groups is an important and highly valued aspect of identity and may be represented/displayed to others through symbols, labels, or ideologies. Therefore, we suggest that clinicians unpack the term "diversity" to understand the role and purpose of social groups for any given individual – what the social groups they belong to give them (in terms of resources, coping) – as well as any negative impacts of such groups (such as judgement, rules). This aligns with the highly idiosyncratic and meaning-based approach taken by our model, focusing explicitly on the ways in which contextual factors influence an individual's understandings of loss and their ways of coping.

People experience loss and change regardless of their socio-cultural background. It is important for clinicians to explore the individual's previous and current ways of coping, their values, and to use Socratic dialogue to help clients find their own answers to their difficulties. We believe that "diverse" people do not experience loss and grief any differently than "non-diverse" people. Notably, these categorisations are based on clinicians' positioning and the cultural distance they create between themselves and clients. We posit that the mechanics of change and experiences of loss are the same across people, but the strategies used to process the change may be different based on the person's socio-cultural background. Below, we present some considerations for clinicians working with loss in the contexts of religion and spirituality, and sexuality and relationships.

Religion and Spirituality

Religion and spirituality are central to many individuals' meaning-making processes, giving a sense of belonging and purpose in life, and bringing hope and solace during times of difficulty (Papaleontiou-Louca, 2021). Religion/spirituality include faith – the personal connection with a transcendental being (Cox, 2009), mysticism – belief in other supernatural phenomena such as ghosts and spirits (Gellman, 2019), and symbolism – the use of rituals, customs, and symbols to bring diverse peoples together, for example during funeral rites (Adamson & Holloway, 2013; Evison, 1990). Religion and spirituality further support mental health, wellbeing, and coping through the formation of a social group and identity (Peek, 2005). Religious/spiritual communities are highly important resources, providing both practical and emotional support for individuals (Alannia, 2016). They create belongingness and togetherness, which are especially important during times of distress or loss where an individual may be feeling incredibly lonely and isolated. The combination of faith, mysticism, and rituals can significantly support individuals' coping with the distress and impact of loss.

In the context of loss, it is important to consider whether and to what extent religion/spirituality play a role in an individual's life. In the example of the meaning-making coping model (Park, 2005) earlier, we presented a faith-based example of how situational meaning-making and global meanings relating to religion can be dissonant in the face of loss. Exploring an individual's religious/spiritual beliefs, how this relates to their experiences of suffering and coping, and linking that to their current experience of loss will help both clinician and client to understand inner conflicts which may potentially act as barriers to change in therapy. For example, if an individual is questioning their faith in God following loss, it would be unhelpful for an uninformed therapist to suggest that the client engages more with prayer or connects with their religious community. Similarly, if an individual is highly spiritual and this has been strengthened in the aftermath of loss, it would be remiss of the clinician to be unaware of this and to neglect to include spiritual practices when discussing coping strategies and resources available to the client.

Given that loss can pose significant questions about people's faith, it is necessary to explore this in a gentle and compassionate way. We suggest that clinicians hold the following question in mind: "What is the best compromise for this person?" Exploring both global and appraised meanings in the context of religion will help clinicians to understand the compromise that the client has created to cope with the loss. However, the first compromise may not be the most useful one. For instance, an individual may have renounced religion in the aftermath of loss – but this may not be helping them, as they may remain conflicted, experiencing guilt, shame, betrayal, and disgust, and also the secondary loss of a religious community who could have supported them during a difficult time. These core emotions are closely linked with an individual's values and beliefs and may lead to the experience of secondary emotions such as anger and sadness which are more readily portrayed or accessed. Clinicians' sensitivity to subtle shifts in language and affect during conversations about religion can guide Socratic questioning, supporting a deeper exploration of faith and its meaning to the individual. In doing so, the clinician and the client can gain a better understanding of the current compromise that has been made, and the best compromise for the person – which will in turn guide the formulation and intervention stages of treatment.

It is well-documented that therapists, especially those trained in the global West, are largely atheist and often trained in models rooted in antitheism (Slife & Whoolery, 2006). Given this, religion/spirituality are often unaddressed in therapy – even though clients may want to discuss this central part of their identity and lived experiences (Anand, 2021). Given this, we encourage clinicians to examine their own personal and professional identities, as well as pre-judgements and biases relating to religion and spirituality. This may be a key topic of discussion in supervision, especially when considering work relating to loss which often surfaces highly existential and spiritual conflicts for clients. Through supervision, clinicians can begin to become aware of their own positioning on the topic of religion/spirituality, and so increase their capacity for having conversations about this with clients. It is often the topics that make us uncomfortable or which we have left unexamined which create blind spots in our clinical practice; bringing active awareness and gentle curiosity to our own internal processes helps us to tolerate that discomfort and to re-establish the axis of self – thus enabling us to remain grounded and to anchor clients through potentially distressing conversations.

Sexuality and Relationships

This is another area of identity and difference which needs to be care-fully considered in the context of loss. Sexuality and relationships hold unique meanings, narratives, and experiences for each individual. The loss of an important person can have a significant impact on a person's values and behaviours in relation to sexuality and relationships – therefore exploring this is key to a thorough assessment of loss and grief. Changes in relationships are expected in the context of loss; a loss creates change in one's social system and hence has relational implications for the indi-vidual. These implications are often unspoken – perhaps due to deep-seated and painful emotions such as shame and guilt. Below we provide a few examples of how sexuality and relationships may be affected in the aftermath of loss.

If an individual has lost their sexual and romantic partner, there is an obvious impact on their sexual and romantic functioning. These physical needs are often left undiscussed, as there are social taboos that make conversations about sex, sexuality, and desire more challenging to broach. The therapeutic space is not exempt from these taboos, which means that sexuality and desire are often neglected in therapy as well as a person's wider social circle. In this example, we assume that the bereaved indi-vidual is someone who enjoys and needs physical touch – tactile feed-back – in order to feel safe and soothed. The loss of their partner means that they do not receive this tactile feedback from anyone else in their life, which leaves them feeling lonely and isolated. The desire for physical intimacy may be experienced in the form of trauma-like tactile flashbacks and memory intrusions, further heightening the individual's distress in the here-and-now.

Of note, the individual may be seeking physical intimacy and sex, but not for romance or love (Diamond, 2003) – phenomena which are often conflated – and yet the stigma from society remains the same. They may fear seeking physical comfort from others due to shame; society tells them that they must not "move on" too quickly; there are negative social consequences for seeking sexual or physically intimate contact with others soon after a loss (Radosh & Simkin, 2016). This is especially true of women, who further contend with gendered views of sexuality and desire

(Crawford & Popp, 2003). It is also true of older people: there is a common ageist assumption that those who are older do not have sexual desires or physical needs (Rheaume & Mitty, 2008). Furthermore, the loss of a sexual/romantic partner may bring to the fore pre-existing dilemmas about gender identity (Díaz-Andreu, 2007), sexual identity (Dillon et al., 2011), or romantic identity which may add to the distress of the loss itself.

Another example is that of the loss of a child (Dyregrov & Gjestad, 2011). There may be conflicting emotions – as with the example above – of wanting physical intimacy without sex. There may also be a complete denial of any physical pleasure or desire as to experience this would heighten feelings of guilt. Individuals may hold socially informed values and beliefs about what it means to seek and experience pleasure in the context of loss. They may have judgements about the "right" and "wrong" ways to act in this situation which constrain their actions and may conflict with their embodied experiences. Individuals who have lost a child and still feel a physical desire for sex may feel disgust towards the self for having those desires at all – and these are likely to be negative judgements and emotions which they do not discuss with anyone. Therefore, neglecting to enquire about sexuality and relationships can lead to huge blind spots in the clinician's understandings of an individual's pain in the aftermath of loss.

Responses to Disasters and the Coronavirus Pandemic

Disasters

This section focuses on strategies to increase resilience and support well-being following a widespread disaster. Given the timing of this publication, we attempt to offer a series of considerations for clinicians working during the coronavirus pandemic with the hope that this guidance may be applicable to other contexts in which individuals and communities face disaster and fatal outcomes.

Hobfoll et al. (2007) consulted with a worldwide panel of experts and reviewed the key needs that must be met following disasters; whilst their focus was explicitly on disaster, the principles remain applicable to the situation in which we find ourselves during the pandemic and the aftermath of Coronavirus (COVID-19). Hobfoll et al. (2007) found five empirically supported intervention principles for early- to mid-term stages post-disaster. Firstly, they suggested that working on psychological distress may not be appropriate (and may, in fact, be harmful) immediately after the distressing event. Additional psychological support would only be indicated where individuals continue to experience physiological and emotional symptoms of distress in the longer term. Hobfoll et al. (2007) warn against rigid prescription of specific interventions, as each disaster and each individual's and community's responses are unique and are not necessarily pathological. Responses to disaster are often protective and adaptive attempts to cope and survive, and as such need to be understood within this evolutionary context. Moreover, the majority of people are more likely to need support and provision of resources to ease the transition to normalcy (or new normalcy) rather than a diagnosis and clinical intervention. Hobfoll et al. (2007) suggest that clinicians remain mindful of the core principles that can promote recovery and wellbeing rather than focusing on diagnosis or prescriptive intervention.

Hobfoll et al. (2007) referred to the five key principles that caregivers/ employers/ individuals need to promote in order to aid recovery from significant, and potentially distressing, events. The key principles are: sense of safety, calming, self-efficacy and collective efficacy, and connectedness and hope. The primary principle following any disaster or a significant event, would be the development of a sense of safety. It is important to recognise that there will be a persistent sense of threat for some time, therefore the best focus would be to create or increase a sense of relative safety. One of the primary concerns would be the development of an actual (physical) safe place, leading to the potential for creating positive feelings and emotional and psychological safety. This requires top-down management of safety by the government, such as the explanation of efforts made to manage public expectations and understandings of threats and public health strategies. For example, individuals seek clarity about the safety of children in school, or about their own safety at work. Addressing this requires public health organisations to provide empathy towards and normalisation of the population's experiences of anxiety, worry, and low mood. Leading by example, public health messages need to emphasise the importance of considering the wellbeing of both the self and others, focusing on community and population health as arising from the contributions of individual citizens. These strategies are likely to facilitate calming, connectedness, and foster collective efficacy and hope; taken together, this would increase the felt sense of safety in both individuals and communities.

Specific interventions offered must address anxiety, worry, and low mood; offering short-term skills development such as distress management and emotion regulation interventions is likely to increase self-efficacy. Additionally, encouraging engagement with positive activities which bring feelings of joy, humour, interest, and contentment is likely to foster self-efficacy and safety. Further interventions encouraging community organising and highlighting the supportive role that communities can play during times of disaster are likely to mitigate perceptions of vulnerability, counteract isolation and loneliness, and foster connectedness, collective efficacy, and hope. In the context of education, UNESCO and others (UNESCO et al., 2021) have recognised the restoration of school communities as being an essential cornerstone to re-establishing a sense of self-efficacy in children and adolescents. This occurs through renewed learning opportunities, engagement in age-appropriate adult-guided memorial rit-uals, and pro-social activities.

Other considerations include helping individuals link in with friends, loved ones, or groups who are positive and helpful. There is a need to increase the quality, quantity, and frequency of supportive transactions. In addition, the development of communities such as school or work using a "mini village" approach – with councils, meeting places, entertainment, recreational activities, mentoring, and solidarity activities is recommended. There is also a need to proactively address potential negative social influences such as mistrust, in- and out-group dynamics, impatience with rates of recovery, and a sense of exhaustion. It is recommended that public health practitioners consider encouraging the populace to identify and engage with those who lack strong systems at home: for example, to provide support for others, such as by being a good listener, a good friend, and encouraging others to seek formal support when needed. These interventions are likely to improve connectedness, collective effi-cacy, and provide a sense of calming and safety both for the individual and the community.

Another approach would be to collaborate with communities that pro-vide support and hope during times of distress, such as religious and spiritual organisations. Utilising these pre-existing social networks and support systems to disseminate messages about the likely changes to daily living as a consequence of disaster can help individuals and com-munities to manage their expectations and to focus on current needs and future-oriented goals. It is important to encourage communities to focus on fact-based thinking which does not rely on catastrophisation of current circumstances and to review and renew motivations for learning and future planning. It would be useful to encourage communities to focus on being present in the here-and-now through spiritual and religious rituals and practices to shift them away from rumination and worry, which serve only to heighten and maintain distress. Similarly, religious and spiritual com-munities offer platforms for the dissemination of psychoeducation about mental health, wellbeing, and coping – and may enable many people to receive psychological support whom mental healthcare services do not typically reach.

These five core elements outlined by Hobfoll et al. (2007) apply to indi-viduals and communities (such as the school community and places of work) and there are many ways to operationalise these principles. The above considerations for supporting individual and collective wellbeing need to be implemented and maintained over time, ideally until a period of relative stability is achieved. Once this has occurred, individuals are likely to be more willing and able to engage with the processing of their specific experiences of loss in one-to-one therapy as set out in the remainder of this book. We acknowledge that many clinicians may not have the resources or capability to intervene at the community- or systems levels outlined earlier. Nonetheless, we encourage readers to reflect on their own experiences of loss in the context of pandemic and disaster as a first step towards developing skills of reflexivity independently and in supervision. We also recommend that this is included in formulations of clients' experiences of loss, with a specific focus on loss-as-change and the changes wrought by the pandemic for the client at the individual, relational, and community levels of functioning.

Pandemic

We experience both expected and unexpected losses; some events are assumed as likely to occur, whereas others can be unimaginable. For example, the ending of a difficult romantic relationship with long-standing conflict and arguments may be expected. Similarly, the loss of a parent after chronic illness and hospitalisation may be expected. On the other hand, some losses are completely unexpected. For example, losing a child who ended their own life may be an unanticipated loss if the parent was unaware of the challenges their child was navigating. On a larger scale, the COVID-19 pandemic has created a huge amount and variety of unexpected loss of many people all around the world. The impact of COVID has been immense for people living in different communities and countries all over the planet. Whilst this doesn't necessarily make things easier, it confirms that the threat is not localised/targeted to one individual and can bring a sense of community and joint suffering.

The ongoing nature of the pandemic since early 2020 has also led to some changes: in the beginning, the pandemic itself was unexpected and there was a sense of invincibility for most people – therefore losing the people they loved to COVID came as a surprise. Over time, the pandemic has taken so many lives, and so many people have tested positive or developed symptoms, that this has almost become mundane – expected. People all over the planet have come to be attuned to hearing about COVID-related risks and losses, to the extent that the huge numbers of daily hospitalisations and deaths no longer hold the weight and impact that they did in 2020. We can think of this as a fear response attuned to threat and safekeeping, that has attenuated over time. Again, this can be linked to the idea that whilst we are all aware of our own mortality, holding this constantly in the forefront of the mind is both intensely distressing and likely unsustainable in the long term. Therefore, we have developed different ways to cope with the ongoing threat of the pandemic such that we are not constantly overwhelmed by a fear of death – our own or others' – and can continue to function as much as possible within our lives. Of course, for some people this sense of threat may not have attenuated, and they may have developed a presentation consistent with generalised anxiety disorder, obsessive-compulsive disorder, or health anxiety – labelled recently as "coronaphobia" (Arora et al., 2020). Relatedly, for those individuals who experienced severe and multiple personal losses as a result of the pandemic, their presentation may be more aligned with that of learned helplessness, or PTSD.

When we experience multiple losses, the meaning made differs based on the type of event. When there is a threat felt by the majority of people, there is increased focus on the cause and effect. If the cause was natural (e.g. tsunami), there is less anger directed towards the event itself (being angry at a tsunami is futile), and greater experience of unfairness – Why me? Why us? Why now? On the other hand, when the threat is human-made, the target of anger is the specific people/group/nation seen to be causing the pain. Some disasters are more acceptable than others – the interpretation of the event and the direction of the anger is different for natural disasters in comparison to human-made events for example wars. This has a significant impact on the ways in which people are able to accept that the event has happened, assimilate the meaning of the event into their worldview, and to move towards functionality in their daily life.

If the cause of the loss is due to natural phenomena (e.g. floods) it may be more likely to be ascribed as an act of God; conversely, losses caused by human-made events (e.g. wars) are more likely to be understood as arising from specific people's/groups' actions. Nonetheless, in both cases there is a feeling of being out of control, and a need to find someone to blame – for someone to take responsibility for what has happened. Such blame is then ascribed to specific people (including oneself) or figures (e.g. political leaders, God) as a way to find a "solution" to the "problem". For example, the COVID-19 pandemic has resulted in a huge loss at the individual, relational, community, societal, and global levels across domains such as emotional connection, education, and economy. There has been a corresponding search for meaning – a search for whom to blame. Whilst initially this "problem" was "solved" through the use of racism to blame Chinese people, over time a shift occurred: instead of blaming the cause of the tragedy, people began to focus on the process of how it was being managed. Therefore, social narratives shifted from racism towards political parties and individual political leaders, and their perceived competence in managing a global pandemic. This drive to find a more powerful person/figure/organisation to take responsibility and to experience the rage of the populace is seen in other contexts where mortality is imminent and anxiety in the system is high (Menzies-Lyth, 1960; Van Der Walt & Swartz, 1999).

It is also important to note that some people consider the COVID-19 pandemic to be a human-made context intended to reduce the human population on the planet. When there are so many unknown variables in relation to COVID, the person trying to find an "answer" to the "problem" is at a loss; there is insufficient information to come to a conclusion. Therefore, they find the most adaptive coping strategies available to them in order to navigate the anxieties of the pandemic. For some individuals, understanding the pandemic as human-made helps them to direct their anger towards specific groups/individuals and may help them to cope with the vast uncertainties of living during the time of a pandemic.

Additionally, we see the impact that natural disasters can have on religion and spirituality; with some people moving closer to God in the aftermath of loss, and others moving away (Aten et al., 2019). The perception of the loss depends on the person – the value and meaning attached is what determines the experience of loss and the process of grieving. In the context of the COVID-19 pandemic, some people's global beliefs about the safety and predictability of the world, and the capacity of God to protect them have been challenged. This has led to a re-evaluation of their global values and beliefs, and for some a movement away from the faith (Park, 2005). For others, it has led to a strengthening of faith, whereby situational appraisals of the threat are amended to be brought in line with global beliefs about the nature of the world and the nature of God (Kowalczyk et al., 2020).

Multiple Losses

In this subsection we consider the impact of multiple losses on an individual's responses and functioning. It is important to note that the context of the losses is important: the meaning someone makes of multiple losses will be different if the losses were caused by natural disasters as opposed to war.

As with any loss, we suggest that the initial response is one of shock and trauma; the person feels frozen in time in relation to what has happened to them. Following this, a survival mechanism kicks in, whereby the person needs to prioritise their own wellbeing, to protect themselves, and reach safety. Once the external threat is reduced to some degree, for example if the individual is able to escape the region of conflict, their mind then re-enters the problem-solving mode. This involves recalling information relating to the losses, which can present similarly to PTSD symptoms, in order to "solve" the "problem" – Why did they have to die? Why did this happen to me? What could I have done to prevent this?

Once this process has begun, there are three possible responses available to the individual: a freeze response, a threat-based response (either fear-based including anxiety and worry, or anger-based involving aggression and irritability), and a learned-helplessness response consisting of sadness, demotivation, and hopelessness. For example, a person who has experienced multiple losses due to natural disaster is likely to be in an initial state of freeze where they try to figure out what is happening and how to survive. This is an automatic/default response that prioritises the individual's safety in order to protect them. Once the individual is out of immediate danger and their life is no longer under threat, they are likely to revisit their experiences in order to make sense of them. This meaning-making process may result in them understanding the disaster as an act of God which was inevitable, and as a test of their faith. This could result in a strengthening of the connection with God and re-commitment to faith. Alternatively, they may focus on the unfairness of the experience and blame an external figure (e.g. God) in order to regulate their emotions. In this scenario, they may become disillusioned with their faith and further distance themselves from religion and/or spirituality.

The main difference between one loss and multiple losses is the difference in the value and function of each relationship that the individual has lost. For example, if a person loses three family members in the same incident, the survivor has to find a way to process that information and find a resolution to those losses. Each of the people they lost would have held a different role in their life; a father is not the same as a mother and neither are the same as a sibling. The individual might unify those losses in order to create meaning – for example, focusing on the cause of the losses in the case of a natural disaster may help them to see these events as part of a "bigger picture" relating to God's plan. On the other hand, in the case of human-made suffering (e.g. war) they may focus more on the process (e.g. being on the run and escaping to a neighbouring area for shelter) rather than on the cause of the losses. Sometimes people value different members of the family differently – for example if someone is closer to their brother than their sister, they may experience a greater impact in relation to the loss of the brother than the sister. The function of each relationship and the degree of closeness will determine the degree to which the individual is distressed by the loss and the resulting impact on their functioning.

Experiencing multiple losses is not the same as a dose–response relationship that is two losses do not lead to double the distress or double the impaired functioning compared to one loss. Each loss is unique, holding specific features (triggers, meanings), and hence each has a different impact on the individual. Sometimes losses feed into each other or are intertwined (e.g. losing both parents), meaning that the loss is kept alive for longer. This makes it harder to come to a sense of resolution more readily, and the whole process becomes onerous because there are additional components of guilt and shame which complicate the experience. For example, an individual may reconcile the loss of their parent by reassuring themselves that "at least they lived a long life". However, when their sibling passes away soon after, this way of understanding loss adds to their distress because their sibling did not live a "long enough" life. In this example, the meaning-making of the first loss has a negative impact on the meaning-making of the second loss. In this way, the impact of each loss subsequently affects the impact of future losses, and this process is mediated by meaning-making. Whilst this is also the case when individual experiences multiple losses spread out over time (e.g. 10 years apart), the impact of losses on each other is greater the closer together they are in time. This is because the individual has not even begun processing the first loss when the second occurs, hence they are caught in the middle of the freeze/threat/helplessness responses in a way that heightens their distress and so prolongs this processing.

A more everyday example of multiple losses can be given here. Let us imagine that you lose your mobile phone, house keys, and car keys at the same time when you are some distance away from home. Your initial response may be to get home first (a place of safety), but then you realise you don't have keys to get in, so that would be fruitless. Each issue is met with a similar barrier: which problem do you solve first? Do you try to solve all three at the same time? Do you prioritise? If so, how? Our minds enter the problem-solving mode immediately – and perhaps as you read this you notice your brain generating various possible solutions to this conundrum! However, the solutions that we try to find are always context-bound: it depends on where you are, what time it is, and what demands you have to meet. Being in this situation in the same neighbour-hood as your house is one thing, but imagine this occurring when you are on holiday in a country where you don't speak the local language. The pri-orities are completely different now. Similarly, if you are a woman on your own when this happens, and it is approaching night-time, that is a very different scenario calling for a very different set of responses in contrast to – for example – being in this scenario as a man in the daytime. Our inter-sectional contexts continually inform our sense of safety and need for pro-tection, and hence organise our thinking to find the most optimal solutions. Therefore, each person confronted with this scenario is likely to come to a different answer. One person may have the thought "someone stole these items from me…what if they steal everything from my house?" and may become preoccupied by hypervigilance and worry. Another person may think "there's no way to get help, I might as well wait here for someone to come along by chance", hence using acceptance as a way to regulate and cope with the uncertainty of the situation. For another person, that same thought of "there's no way to get help" may move them towards a place of helplessness or hopelessness.

In the context of loss, choosing which loss (e.g. which family member) to focus on first is an almost-impossible decision to make. The act of having to choose may itself add to the person's distress and hence make it even harder to process the losses. For individuals living a long way away from family members, the physical distance from the people they have lost and the lack of information can further complicate the grief response. They may stay stuck in the primal responses of trying to solve the problem, wanting more information and clarity about what happened, how their family members died, when, where, and so on. There may be a frantic pull towards gathering as much information as possible, as the not-knowing is too painful to tolerate. However, gaining that information may not bring the cathartic release that the person is hoping for. It is important to consider: Does it help to know more? Does it cause more difficulties? The individual may find that gaining additional factual knowledge about the course of events may only fuel their pain and distress, rather than lessening it. The way this process unfolds of course depends on the individual's characteristics, their coping styles, and previous experiences of loss. Some people may focus on the practical/tangible aspects of the experience (knowing exactly what happened and when) as a way to build a coherent narrative and hence soothe their emotions. For others, focusing on the details may increase distress, so instead they skim over the events to the outcome "what's happened has happened. It can't be changed."

Loss is not just about death – it can be about moving away, being transferred, and so on. This is something that armed forces personnel are likely to experience to a great degree. They may lose friends and colleagues in armed conflict, due to transfer, or when people leave the armed forces entirely. Due to the intense nature of relationships forged in the armed services, the impact of losses of this kind is likely huge and also unnoticed by society. People who have served time in the armed forces may return to civilian life with conflicting feelings, be confronted by a very different way of life that they need to re-adjust to and may also be experiencing the aftermath of multiple losses (Van Staden et al., 2007). Leaving the armed forces following a prolonged period of service may result in feelings of isolation, abandonment, and a lack of clarity about one's direction in life (Duel et al., 2019). This may lead to the person trying to "solve" the "problem" by recalling their experiences in the armed forces, recollecting their losses – perhaps consciously, and perhaps in a trauma-like intrusive manner. Again, after emerging from a state of freeze, they are likely to take one of the three positions: learned helplessness (I get no support from welfare services, I am alone), anger (I have done so much for this country and now I'm ostracised? This is unfair), and fear (I am under threat, I cannot relax or I may die like my friends and colleagues have died).

We can also consider here the anticipation of multiple losses. This is especially pertinent in the context of the COVID-19 pandemic where there is a constant and current worry that people around us are deemed to be more vulnerable – especially in comparison to the self. For instance, we may all be more cautious when visiting elderly relatives, yet we continue to take risks in our daily lives because we do not fear the consequences for ourselves to the same degree. Depending on a person's lived experiences and coping styles, they may be more or less inclined to worry about anticipatory loss in this context. Some people may have a long history of experiencing anxiety and worry, and the COVID-19 context may feed into pre-existing beliefs about the dangers inherent in the world, and their self-perceived inability to cope. This may lead to increased tension and hypervigilance, in relation to their own safety, as well as the safety of others who are important to them. For some people who may already have learned this way of coping in the past, or who were predisposed to this type of coping, these worries may be converted into ritualistic or compulsive behaviours associated with health anxiety and/or OCD. For others who were more predisposed to learned helplessness, the increased isolation enforced by COVID-19 restrictions may result in lower mood, hopelessness, and demotivation in their daily life. Increased government-enforced and self-imposed social isolation may compound this issue, making it more challenging for the individual to cope with losses (both actual and anticipated).

The experience of multiple losses has an impact at both the individual and the collective levels. For example, 96 people died at Hillsborough and hundreds more were injured during a football match in Sheffield in 1989 (Tikkanen, 2021). This was a tragedy at the individual and collective level, due to the interlinked nature of the multiple losses – the people who died had a common interest, were supporters of the same football club, were part of the football community, and also a part of their respective social networks and local communities. The impact at each of these levels is different, and yet overlapping as each influences the next. The way that people understand the event that occurred influences how the community as a whole and society at that time made sense of it. It seems that the incident was largely blamed on the police at the time; this is likely to be a broader socio-cultural narrative that arose out of the process and aftermath of the event (Shenhav, 2015). It may then also have influenced individual meaning-making such that the collective understands the loss as occurring due to the fault of an outside agency (the police). This holds a protective function for the collective and the individual: placing the responsibility and blame on the out-group (Tajfel et al., 1979) can create distance from the event, whilst enabling the processing of painful emotions such as anger and sadness about the losses experienced.

Summary

Loss is inevitable, as is grief; the grieving process has been much-studied, but a clear CBT-based approach for working with loss has not yet been proposed. We outline here a novel framework based that can be used to re-balance the socio-occupational and emotional functioning of individuals who have experienced loss. This model incorporates elements of classic CBT, TF-CBT, CFT, metacognitive awareness, and ACT to guide individuals through the grieving process, with the explicit aim of increasing their functioning, rather than focusing on reducing their (superficial) symptoms.

The remainder of this guide will focus on the way in which to implement this model therapeutically. Chapter 2 provides an overview of the assessment process, Chapter 3 describes formulation and case conceptualisation, and Chapter 4 provides guidance for clinical intervention, and Chapter 5 outlines supervision content and process.

References

Abramson, L. Y., Seligman, M. E., & Teasdale, J. D. (1978). Learned helplessness in humans: Critique and reformulation. *Journal of Abnormal Psychology*, *87*(1), 49.

Adamson, S., & Holloway, M. (2013). Symbols and symbolism in the funeral today: What do they tell us about contemporary spirituality? *Journal for the Study of Spirituality*, *3*(2), 140–155.

Ainsworth, M. D. S., Blehar, M. C., Waters, E., & Wall, S. N. (2015). *Patterns of attachment: A psychological study of the strange situation*. Psychology Press.

Akannia, A. (2016). Mechanism for coping with moments of grief in Islam. *Sociology*, *6*(10), 663–675.

Alsop-Shields, L., & Mohay, H. (2001). John Bowlby and James Robertson: Theorists, scientists and crusaders for improvements in the care of children in hospital. *Journal of Advanced Nursing*, *35*(1), 50–58.

Anand, N. (2021). *Religious meaning-making in individual psychotherapy*. [Doctoral Thesis]. UCL.

APA. (2013). *Diagnostic and statistical manual of mental disorders (DSM-5)*.

Arora, A., Jha, A. K., Alat, P., & Das, S. S. (2020). Understanding coronaphobia. *Asian Journal of Psychiatry*, *54*, 102384.

Aten, J. D., Smith, W. R., Davis, E. B., Van Tongeren, D. R., Hook, J. N., Davis, D. E., Shannonhouse, L., DeBlaere, C., Ranter, J., & O'Grady, K. (2019). The psychological study of religion and spirituality in a disaster context: A systematic review. *Psychological Trauma: Theory, Research, Practice, and Policy*, *11*(6), 597.

Barrett, L. F. (2012). Emotions are real. *Emotion*, *12*(3), 413.

Beck, A. (2016). *Transcultural cognitive behaviour therapy for anxiety and depression: A practical guide*. Routledge.

Beck, A. T. (1979). *Cognitive therapy of depression*. Guilford Press.

Berry, J. W. (2003). *Conceptual approaches to acculturation*. American Psychological Association.

Bonanno, G. A., Wortman, C. B., Lehman, D. R., Tweed, R. G., Haring, M., Sonnega, J., Carr, D., & Nesse, R. M. (2002). Resilience to loss and chronic grief: A prospective study from preloss to 18-months postloss. *Journal of Personality and Social Psychology*, *83*(5), 1150.

Bourne, C., Mackay, C., & Holmes, E. A. (2013). The neural basis of flashback formation: The impact of viewing trauma. *Psychological Medicine*, *43*(7), 1521–1532.

Bowlby, J. (1963). Pathological mourning and childhood mourning. *Journal of the American Psychoanalytic Association*, *11*(3), 500–541.

Boyer, P., & Bergstrom, B. (2011). Threat-detection in child development: An evolutionary perspective. *Neuroscience & Biobehavioral Reviews*, *35*(4), 1034–1041.

Bracha, H. S. (2004). Freeze, flight, fight, fright, faint: Adaptationist perspectives on the acute stress response spectrum. *CNS Spectrums*, *9*(9), 679–685.

Brewin, C. R., & Holmes, E. A. (2003). Psychological theories of posttraumatic stress disorder. *Clinical Psychology Review, 23*(3), 339–376.

Brown, H. (2018). Reciprocal roles in an unequal world. In J. Lloyd & R. Pollard (Eds.), *Cognitive analytic therapy and the politics of mental health* (pp. 20–37). Routledge.

Burnham, J. (2018). Developments in social GRRRAAACCEEESSS: Visible–invisible and voiced–unvoiced 1. In I.-B. Krause (Ed.), *Culture and reflexivity in systemic psychotherapy* (pp. 139–160). Routledge.

Carey, T. A., & Stiles, W. B. (2016). Some problems with randomized controlled trials and some viable alternatives. *Clinical Psychology & Psychotherapy, 23*(1), 87–95.

Cox, H. (2009). *The future of faith*. Harper One.

Cozzolino, P. J., Blackie, L. E., & Meyers, L. S. (2014). Self-related consequences of death fear and death denial. *Death Studies, 38*(6), 418–422.

Crawford, M., & Popp, D. (2003). Sexual double standards: A review and methodological critique of two decades of research. *Journal of Sex Research, 40*(1), 13–26.

Darwin, C. (1859). *On the origin of species by means of natural selection, or the preservation of favoured races in the struggle for life*. John Murray.

De Waal, F. B. (2008). Putting the altruism back into altruism: The evolution of empathy. *Annual Review of Psychology, 59*, 279–300.

Diamond, L. M. (2003). What does sexual orientation orient? A biobehavioral model distinguishing romantic love and sexual desire. *Psychological Review, 110*(1), 173.

Díaz-Andreu, M. (2007). *Gender identity*. Routledge.

Dillon, F. R., Worthington, R. L., & Moradi, B. (2011). Sexual identity as a universal process. In S. J. Schwartz, K. Luyckx, & V. L. Vignoles (Eds.), *Handbook of identity theory and research* (pp. 649–670). Springer.

Duel, J., Godier-McBard, L., MacLean, M. B., & Fossey, M. (2019). Challenging missions: Vulnerable Veterans leaving the armed forces and promising avenues to support them. In C. Castro & S. Dursun (Eds.), *Military veteran reintegration: approach, management, and assessment of military veterans transitioning to civilian life* (pp. 95–134). Academic Press.

Dyregrov, A., & Gjestad, R. (2011). Sexuality following the loss of a child. *Death Studies, 35*(4), 289–315.

Ehlers, A., & Clark, D. M. (2000). A cognitive model of posttraumatic stress disorder. *Behaviour Research and Therapy, 38*(4), 319–345.

Evison, G. G. A. (1990). *Indian death rituals*. University of Oxford.

Feeny, N. C., Zoellner, L. A., Fitzgibbons, L. A., & Foa, E. B. (2000). Exploring the roles of emotional numbing, depression, and dissociation in PTSD. *Journal of Traumatic Stress, 13*(3), 489–498.

Fonagy, P. (2001). *Attachment theory and psychoanalysis*. Other Press, LLC.

Freud, S. (1957). Mourning and melancholia. In L. G. Fiorini, T. Bokanowski, & S. Lewkowicz (Eds.), *The standard edition of the complete psychological works of Sigmund Freud, Volume XIV (1914–1916): On the history of the psychoanalytic movement, papers on metapsychology and other works* (pp. 237–258). Routledge.

Freud, S., & Strachey, J. E. (1964). *The standard edition of the complete psychological works of Sigmund Freud*. Macmillan.

Gellman, J. (2019). Mysticism. In E. N. Zalta (Ed.), *The Stanford encyclopedia of philosophy* (Vol. Summer). https://plato.stanford.edu/archives/sum2019/entries/mysticism/.

Gilbert, P. (2007). The evolution of shame as a marker for relationship security: A biopsychosocial approach. In J. L. Tracy, R. W. Robins, & J. P. Tangney (Eds.), *The self-conscious emotions: Theory and research* (pp. 283–309). Guilford Press.

Gilbert, P. (2010). *The compassionate mind: A new approach to life's challenges*. London: Constable.

Gilbert, P. (2014). Social mentalities: Internal "social" conflict and the role of inner warmth and compassion in cognitive therapy. In P. Gilbert & K. G. Bailey (Eds.), *Genes on the couch* (pp. 128–160). Routledge.

Gilbert, P. (2016). *Human nature and suffering*. Routledge.

Goffman, E. (1959). *1959 The presentation of self in everyday life*. Doubleday.

Hall, C. (2014). Bereavement theory: Recent developments in our understanding of grief and bereavement. *Bereavement Care, 33*(1), 7–12.

Harris, R. (2019). *ACT made simple: An easy-to-read primer on acceptance and commitment therapy*. New Harbinger Publications.

Hartman, C. R., & Burgess, A. W. (1993). Information processing of trauma. *Child Abuse & Neglect, 17*(1), 47–58.

Hashempour, F. (2008). *Cultural Distance* [Educational Presentation]. International conference of cognitive psychotherapy (ICCP), June 2011 Istanbul. Workshop title: "Thinking differently about difference: delivering effective CBT interventions to diverse populations".

Hashempour, F. (2016). *Use of cognitive measurement tools in prediction of psychological wellbeing*. [Doctoral Thesis]. Institute for Health Research – University of Bedfordshire.

Hayes, S. C., Strosahl, K. D., & Wilson, K. G. (2009). *Acceptance and commitment therapy*. American Psychological Association.

Hays, P. A. (2008). *Addressing cultural complexities in practice*. American Psychological Association.

Hermanto, N., & Zuroff, D. C. (2016). The social mentality theory of self-compassion and self-reassurance: The interactive effect of care-seeking and caregiving. *Journal of Social Psychology, 156*(5), 523–535.

Hobfoll, S. E., Watson, P., Bell, C. C., Bryant, R. A., Brymer, M. J., Friedman, M. J., Friedman, M., Gersons, B. P., De Jong, J. T., & Layne, C. M. (2007). Five essential elements of immediate and mid-term mass trauma intervention: Empirical evidence. *Psychiatry: Interpersonal and Biological Processes, 70*(4), 283–315.

Holmes, J. (2014). *John Bowlby and attachment theory*. Routledge.

Howarth, R. (2011). Concepts and controversies in grief and loss. *Journal of Mental Health Counseling, 33*(1), 4–10.

Jackson, D. P. (1997). *The epic of Gilgamesh*. Bolchazy-Carducci Publishers.

Johnson, J. (2022). *Honoring grief with your whole heart*. Healing Healthcare: A Global Mindfulness Summit.

Kilner, J. M., & Lemon, R. N. (2013). What we know currently about mirror neurons. *Current Biology, 23*(23), R1057–R1062.

Klass, D., Silverman, P. R., & Nickman, S. (2014). *Continuing bonds: New understandings of grief*. Taylor & Francis.

Knipe, J. (2009). Shame is my safe place. In R. Shapiro (Ed.), *EMDR Solutions II: For Depression, Eating Disorders, Performance, and More*. Norton Professional Books.

Kowalczyk, O., Roszkowski, K., Montane, X., Pawliszak, W., Tylkowski, B., & Bajek, A. (2020). Religion and faith perception in a pandemic of COVID-19. *Journal of Religion and Health, 59*(6), 2671–2677.

Kubler-Ross, E. (1969). *On death and dying*. Routledge.

Lang, P. J., Bradley, M. M., & Cuthbert, B. N. (1990). Emotion, attention, and the startle reflex. *Psychological Review, 97*(3), 377.

Lazarus, R. S. (1984). On the primacy of cognition. *American Psychologist, 39*(2), 124–129.

Lazarus, R. S. (2000). Evolution of a model of stress, coping, and discrete emotions. In V. H. Rice (Ed.), *Handbook of stress, coping, and health: Implications for nursing research, theory, and practice*, 195–222. SAGE Publications.

Lazarus, R. S., & Folkman, S. (1987). Transactional theory and research on emotions and coping. *European Journal of Personality, 1*(3), 141–169.

Malkinson, R. (2007). *Cognitive grief therapy: Constructing a rational meaning to life following loss*. WW Norton.

Malkinson, R. (2010). Cognitive-behavioral grief therapy: The ABC model of rational-emotion behavior therapy. *Psihologijske Teme, 19*(2), 289–305.

Malkinson, R., Rubin, S. S., & Witztum, E. (2006). Therapeutic issues and the relationship to the deceased: Working clinically with the two-track model of bereavement. *Death Studies, 30*(9), 797–815.

McKinlay, A. P. (1924). Cicero's letters. *Texas Review, 9*(2), 113–132.

McLean, K. C., Pasupathi, M., & Pals, J. L. (2007). Selves creating stories creating selves: A process model of self-development. *Personality and Social Psychology Review, 11*(3), 262–278.

Menzies-Lyth, I. (1960). A case-study in the functioning of social systems as a defence against anxiety. *Human Relations, 13*(1), 95–121.

Morris, S. (2018). *Overcoming grief 2nd edition: A self-help guide using cognitive behavioural techniques*. Hachette UK.

Neimeyer, R. A. (2000). Searching for the meaning of meaning: Grief therapy and the process of reconstruction. *Death Studies, 24*(6), 541–558.

Nesse, R. M. (1994). Fear and fitness: An evolutionary analysis of anxiety disorders. *Ethology and Sociobiology, 15*(5–6), 247–261.

Oswald, M. E., & Grosjean, S. (2004). Confirmation bias. In *Cognitive illusions: A handbook on fallacies and biases in thinking, judgement and memory*, 79. Psychology Press. https://doi. org/10.13140/2.1, 2068

Papaleontiou-Louca, E. (2021). Effects of religion and faith on mental health. *New Ideas in Psychology, 60*, e100833–e100833.

Park, C. L. (2005). Religion as a meaning making framework in coping with life stress. *Journal of Social Issues, 61*(4), 707–729.

Peek, L. (2005). Becoming Muslim: The development of a religious identity. *Sociology of Religion, 66*(3), 215–242.

Power, M. J., & Dalgleish, T. (1999). Two routes to emotion: Some implications of multi-level theories of emotion for therapeutic practice. *Behavioural and Cognitive Psychotherapy, 27*(2), 129–141.

Pyszczynski, T., Greenberg, J., Solomon, S., & Maxfield, M. (2006). On the unique psychological import of the human awareness of mortality: Theme and variations. *Psychological Inquiry, 17*(4), 328–356.

Radosh, A., & Simkin, L. (2016). Acknowledging sexual bereavement: A path out of disenfranchised grief. *Reproductive Health Matters, 24*(48), 25–33.

Rheaume, C., & Mitty, E. (2008). Sexuality and intimacy in older adults. *Geriatric Nursing, 29*(5), 342–349.

Rollnick, S., Butler, C. C., Kinnersley, P., Gregory, J., & Mash, B. (2010). Motivational interviewing. *Annual Review of Clinical Psychology, 1*(1), 91–111.

Rostila, M., & Saarela, J. M. (2011). Time does not heal all wounds: Mortality following the death of a parent. *Journal of Marriage and Family, 73*(1), 236–249.

Rubin, S. S., Bar Nadav, O., Malkinson, R., Koren, D., Goffer-Shnarch, M., & Michaeli, E. (2009). The Two-Track Model of Bereavement Questionnaire (TTBQ): Development and validation of a relational measure. *Death Studies, 33*(4), 305–333.

Rutter, M. (1979). Separation experiences: A new look at an old topic. *Journal of Pediatrics, 95*(1), 147–154.

Sagliano, L., Cappuccio, A., Trojano, L., & Conson, M. (2014). Approaching threats elicit a freeze-like response in humans. *Neuroscience Letters, 561*, 35–40.

Schmidt, N. B., Richey, J. A., Zvolensky, M. J., & Maner, J. K. (2008). Exploring human freeze responses to a threat stressor. *Journal of Behavior Therapy and Experimental Psychiatry, 39*(3), 292–304.

Schraw, G. (1998). Promoting general metacognitive awareness. *Instructional Science, 26*(1), 113–125.

Schraw, G., & Moshman, D. (1995). Metacognitive theories. *Educational Psychology Review, 7*(4), 351–371.

Schuengel, C., Oosterman, M., & Sterkenburg, P. S. (2009). Children with disrupted attachment histories: Interventions and psychophysiological indices of effects. *Child and Adolescent Psychiatry and Mental Health, 3*(1), 1–10.

Schut, H., & Stroebe, M. (1999). The dual process model of coping with bereavement: Rationale and description. *Death Studies, 23*(3), 197–224.

Seligman, M. E. (1972). Learned helplessness. *Annual Review of Medicine, 23*(1), 407–412.

Shakespeare, W. (1599–1601). *Hamlet*. Penguin Classics.

Shakespeare, W. (1608). *King Lear*. Quarto.

Shapiro, F. (2017). *Eye movement desensitization and reprocessing (EMDR) therapy: Basic principles, protocols, and procedures*. Guilford Publications.

Shapiro, F., & Laliotis, D. (2011). EMDR and the adaptive information processing model: Integrative treatment and case conceptualization. *Clinical Social Work Journal, 39*(2), 191–200.

Shear, K., Frank, E., Houck, P. R., & Reynolds, C. F. (2005). Treatment of complicated grief: A randomized controlled trial. *JAMA, 293*(21), 2601–2608.

Shear, M. K., Frank, E., Foa, E., Cherry, C., Reynolds III, C. F., Vander Bilt, J., & Masters, S. (2001). Traumatic grief treatment: A pilot study. *American Journal of Psychiatry, 158*(9), 1506–1508.

Shear, M. K., Reynolds, C. F., Simon, N. M., Zisook, S., Wang, Y., Mauro, C., Duan, N., Lebowitz, B., & Skritskaya, N. (2016). Optimizing treatment of complicated grief: A randomized clinical trial. *JAMA Psychiatry*, *73*(7), 685–694.

Shear, M. K., Wang, Y., Skritskaya, N., Duan, N., Mauro, C., & Ghesquiere, A. (2014). Treatment of complicated grief in elderly persons: A randomized clinical trial. *JAMA Psychiatry*, *71*(11), 1287–1295.

Shenhav, S. R. (2015). *Analyzing social narratives*. Routledge.

Simon, N. M. (2013). Treating complicated grief. *JAMA*, *310*(4), 416–423.

Skinner, B. F. (1965). *Science and human behavior*. Simon and Schuster.

Slife, B. D., & Whoolery, M. (2006). Are psychology's main methods biased against the worldview of many religious people? *Journal of Psychology and Theology*, *34*(3), 217–231.

Smith, A. (2006). Cognitive empathy and emotional empathy in human behavior and evolution. *Psychological Record*, *56*(1), 3–21.

Stein, D. J., & Nesse, R. M. (2011). Threat detection, precautionary responses, and anxiety disorders. *Neuroscience & Biobehavioral Reviews*, *35*(4), 1075–1079.

Stickley, P. R. (2014). *Grief in the Iliad*. Undergraduate Honors Theses. Paper 205. https://dc.etsu.edu/honors/205

Stovall, K. C., & Dozier, M. (1998). Infants in foster care: An attachment theory perspective. *Adoption Quarterly*, *2*(1), 55–88.

Stroebe, W., Zech, E., Stroebe, M. S., & Abakoumkin, G. (2005). Does social support help in bereavement? *Journal of Social and Clinical Psychology*, *24*(7), 1030–1050.

Tajfel, H., Turner, J. C., Austin, W. G., & Worchel, S. (1979). An integrative theory of intergroup conflict. *Organizational Identity: A Reader*, *56*(65), 9780203505984-9780203505916.

Tikkanen, A. (2021). Hillsborough disaster. In *Encyclopedia Britannica*. www.britannica.com/event/Hillsborough-disaster.

Tracy, J. L., Mercadante, E., Witkower, Z., & Cheng, J. T. (2020). The evolution of pride and social hierarchy. In B. Gawronski (Ed.), *Advances in experimental social psychology* (Vol. 62, pp. 51–114). Elsevier.

Triandis, H. C. (2018). *Individualism and collectivism*. Routledge.

UNESCO, UNICEF, WorldBank, WorldFoodProgramme, & UNHCR. (2021). *Framework for Reopening Schools*. UNESDOC Digital Library.

Van Der Walt, H., & Swartz, L. (1999). Isabel Menzies Lyth revisited institutional defences in public health nursing in South Africa during the 1990s. *Psychodynamic Counselling*, *5*(4), 483–495.

van Deurzen, E., Craig, E., Längle, A., Schneider, K. J., Tantam, D., & du Plock, S. (2019). *The Wiley world handbook of existential therapy*. Wiley.

Van Staden, L., Fear, N. T., Iversen, A. C., French, C. E., Dandeker, C., & Wessely, S. (2007). Transition back into civilian life: A study of personnel leaving the UK armed forces via "military prison". *Military Medicine*, *172*(9), 925–930.

Veale, D., Gilbert, P., Wheatley, J., & Naismith, I. (2015). A new therapeutic community: Development of a compassion-focussed and contextual behavioural environment. *Clinical Psychology & Psychotherapy*, *22*(4), 285–303.

Walker, K. N., MacBride, A., & Vachon, M. L. (1977). Social support networks and the crisis of bereavement. *Social Science & Medicine (1967)*, *11*(1), 35–41.

Watkins, A. (2015). *Why You Feel What You Feel*. YouTube. www.youtube.com/watch?v=h-rRgpPbR5w.

Wetherell, J. L. (2012). Complicated grief therapy as a new treatment approach. *Dialogues in Clinical Neuroscience, 14*(2), 159.

Williams, W. I. (2006). Complex trauma: Approaches to theory and treatment. *Journal of Loss and Trauma, 11*(4), 321–335.

Woody, E. Z., & Szechtman, H. (2011). Adaptation to potential threat: The evolution, neurobiology, and psychopathology of the security motivation system. *Neuroscience & Biobehavioral Reviews, 35*(4), 1019–1033.

Worden, J. W. (2018). *Grief counseling and grief therapy: A handbook for the mental health practitioner*. Springer.

Young, I. T., Iglewicz, A., Glorioso, D., Lanouette, N., Seay, K., Ilapakurti, M., & Zisook, S. (2012). Suicide bereavement and complicated grief. *Dialogues in Clinical Neuroscience, 14*(2), 177.

Zajonc, R. B. (1984). On the primacy of affect. *American Psychologist, 39*(2), 117–123. https://doi.org/10.1037/0003-066X.39.2.117

Chapter 2

Assessment

Overview

This chapter focuses on the method and process of assessing clients who have experienced loss, in order to understand their unique meaning-making processes, and develop a formulation to inform therapeutic intervention. As this book is targeted to clinicians with a foundation in cognitive behavioural therapy (CBT) theory and practice, this chapter will not detail the basics of assessment approaches or techniques. Instead, we provide an overview of the application of assessment skills to loss and grief, based on the theoretical framework outlined in Chapter 1. Therefore, we begin this chapter with the assumption that the reader is familiar with the ways in which to introduce therapy, obtain informed consent, and the development of a trusting and collaborative therapeutic relationship through openness, curiosity, and empathy.

It is important to note that topics of loss and grief can generate triggers and points of emotional reference for both clinician and client; therapists are humans too and may experience distress when confronted by this topic. Therefore, when working with loss and grief, it is paramount for clinicians to consider and practice self-care – a topic that we will cover in greater detail in the final chapter of this book. Additionally, it is important to be mindful of the shortfalls in assessment, which may occur due to a number of factors such as time limitations, difficulties in engaging with the topic, abreaction, intrusions, detachment, or many other presentations that could lead to an inconsolable and desolate presentation. Similarly, the process could be seamless and without any difficulties leading to a positive and clear formulation of the loss and grief. We continue this chapter under the assumption that the reader will seek support in developing a strong therapeutic relationship through further reading and supervision as required.

This chapter begins with a brief account of the assessment method; Chapter 3 will focus on using this information to develop an appropriate formulation and treatment plan based on the client's idiosyncratic needs.

DOI: 10.4324/9781003214045-2

When planning an assessment of loss and grief, the primary questions to consider are: (1) What am I investigating? and (2) How will this assessment enable me and the client to develop a helpful formulation of the difficulties they currently face? The main intention of the clinician is to gather information in order to develop a formulation that relates to the client's difficulties ranging from their view of the experience of loss, the feelings associated with that experience, the degree of change in their functioning, and the impact of the loss on their life. Exploring this involves asking questions relating to the individual's prior encounters with loss and the grieving process, their thinking styles, perception and attention, degree of control, and coping skills are crucial to this work. These are the factors that have a clear and direct correlation with the individual's ability to manage, cope with, recover or restore with the loss. Therefore, the crux of the assessment is to investigate and understand how the loss leads to a sense of grief, resulting in an individual becoming a prisoner to their own fear, hatred, blame, shame, and self-criticism.

There are a number of key issues when considering exploration and examination of loss. Pearlman et al. (2014) provide a second-wave CBT approach to assessing, formulating, and treating loss that is based on current symptomatology. Whilst we cover similar ground in the Generic Assessment Section below, our model expands on the work of Pearlman et al. in the Specific Assessment Section. The major difference between the approach recommended by Pearlman et al. and our novel approach presented in this book is our shift away from symptoms and towards functionality. We encourage readers to re-focus their attention onto the functional impairment caused by loss and by the symptoms associated with loss, rather than on those symptoms themselves.

Pearlman et al. (2014) suggest that there are multiple factors affected by loss – which they term "secondary loss", including changes to emotion, physical health, identity, beliefs about the world, relationships, finances, daily living, and hopes and dreams. In our model, we build on this to consider motivation for change and the client's reasoning for that motivation (or lack thereof). This initial discussion will provide an overview of the work to be done and the best approach for that individual client. It is essential to enable the individual to be heard and understood in order to establish a collaborative ground to move forward.

Similar to a formal CBT assessment, the features that require information gathering include predisposing, precipitating, presenting, maintaining, and protective factors (5Ps formulation; Macneil et al., 2012). The opening questions are crucial in establishing initial access to the individual's lived experience, in order to further proceed to the structured assessment. Additionally, there is a need for a method of tracking progress or lack thereof; this consideration could be explored by the use of tools in assessing and monitoring progress. Assessment tools include the clinical interview (if required involving others in the family or care network), a functionality measure, self-monitoring, and clinical observation.

We recommend that clinicians use two sessions to complete a thorough assessment: the first session focuses on consent, risk, and a genetic assessment of the individual's presenting difficulties. At the end of the first session, the client is given the Loss and Grief Functionality Questionnaire (LAG-FQ) self-report questionnaire to complete. The second session focuses on the outcomes from the LAG-FQ and builds a specific assessment of the client's functionality in relation to loss. Whilst this is the recommended structure of an assessment, we recognise that not all clinicians will be able to use this format – perhaps due to constraints on resources within NHS teams. If this is the case, we recommend that the following structure is used: consent, risk, LAG-FQ, generic assessment, and specific assessment.

For clinicians who are familiar with a typical CBT-based assessment process, or who have worked with a client on a different presenting difficulty prior to focusing on loss (and therefore have much of the background information collated in a generic assessment), we recommend skipping the first part of this chapter and focusing instead on the Specific Assessment Section.

Loss and Grief Functionality Questionnaire

The LAG-FQ has been developed to complement the conceptualisation, assessment, formulation, and treatment of loss and grief outlined in this book. The full measure is included in Appendix A. Although currently unpublished, the LAG-FQ is being validated by an independent team of researchers at Queen's University Belfast and is due to be published in a peer-reviewed journal in the upcoming months. Clinicians are invited to use the measure provided in Appendix A to support their work using the Principles of Loss model.

The LAG-FQ consists of 13 items relating to diverse elements of an individual's life, from social and emotional factors, to memory, self-concept, and religion/spirituality. Each item is scored on four dimensions: change, awareness, coping, and acceptance. This allows for a rich exploration of the impact of loss on various elements of an individual's life, as well as how they relate to the loss and the functional impact they are currently experiencing as a result of the loss.

Administering the LAG-FQ prior to the specific assessment allows the clinician to gather data from the client relating to multiple areas of their lived experience which may have been impacted by the loss. We recommend using the client's responses to the LAG-FQ items as a jumping-off point for the specific assessment. If loss has affected the person in multiple areas of their life, we need to understand the degree of the impact of loss in terms of their functioning. They might have developed rituals to cope with the loss – so we need to think about the purpose of that behaviour, rather than focusing on the symptoms themselves.

We recommend that clinicians administer the LAG-FQ. If the clinician is confident with generic assessment, we suggest that they skip ahead to the Specific Assessment Section.

Generic Assessment: Clinical Interview and Clinical Observations

Getting to Know the Client: Accounts of General Life and Daily Events

This part of the assessment is typically exploratory in nature, based on gaining an understanding of the client's functionality in the aftermath of loss by asking open questions related to daily activities, sleep patterns, dietary intake, and social activities. The focus is not on the "symptoms" themselves, but on the change in functionality since the loss and the impact that this has on the individual. Example questions include: How long do your daily routines take these days, and how different is that from before the loss? What impact has the loss had on your routines? What situations or triggers do you notice that may be causing you distress? What is your appetite like, and has it changed since the loss? What have you noticed in terms of your ability to focus and concentrate?

Matrix Assessment

We refer to the main bulk of the assessment as a "matrix assessment" as the clinician attempts to understand linkages between stimuli and their effects on emotion, cognition, and physiological responses. We recognise and highlight the fact that responses may differ based on contextual factors that accompany the stimulus. For example, if a person is already feeling stressed and then is asked to do an additional task, their level of distress is compounded, which has a knock-on effect on their cognitive processing, physiological responses, affective response, and behavioural outcomes. However, if they were not feeling stressed in the first instance, their cognitive, physiological, affective, and behavioural responses might be vastly different. The aim of the matrix assessment is to understand this sequence of events that occurs due to the confluence of stimulus and context.

Emotional

We conceptualise emotions, following Alan Watkins, as "energy in motion" (Watkins, 2015) – as patterns of physiological impulses that spontaneously and continuously occur within our bodies in response to both internal and external stimuli. Emotions can be triggered by cues that remind the individual of their loss. This is due to the evolutionary advantage of being able to respond very quickly (emotional responses can often be faster than cognitive appraisals – i.e. feeling scared before knowing why) to threats, and the benefits of being able to remember those threats and respond to them reflexively without requiring slower cognitive processing. Events that occur in the present, such as hearing about someone else passing away in similar circumstances to one's own loss, may trigger emotional re-living experiences.

Not all individuals are able to notice, recognise, and identify their emotions; although we all have affective experiences, not all of us are able to connect with those emotions and label them. Further still, of those individuals who are able to identify their emotions, not all of them are able to draw links between triggers and emotional responses. In the matrix assessment, the clinician's role is to help the client notice and identify both their emotional responses, and the contexts and triggers that precede those emotional responses.

Clinicians may find it helpful to refer to the list of emotions provided by Pearlman et al. (2014) to help clients identify the emotional responses they experience in the present. However, in the context of our model identifying emotions alone is insufficient. In order to complete a thorough matrix assessment, it is important to also consider the motivations and values that underlie each emotional response. This is due to our integration of ACT principles, which emphasise the importance of the values that drive emotional responses and subsequent behaviours. This ACT and values-based approach must be held in mind from the very beginning of the assessment process.

In terms of the assessment, we recommend that clinicians are attuned to the following features:

- Mood changes without triggers
- An increase in tension
- Reports of being numb
- Anger, irritability, or annoyance
- Low in mood, sad, depressed, or despair
- Incongruency in mood or distorted mood
- Dysregulated mood

We recommend that clinicians pay close attention to reports of an emotional "freeze" response, experienced as numbing or disconnectedness. This may suggest that an individual feels "frozen in time", and from an evolutionary perspective, may be the most adaptive and protective emotional state for them at that moment. For individuals who have shifted out of the freeze response, it is likely that they are experiencing one or more of the "five Fs": (freeze), fight, flight, fright, and faint (Bracha, 2004). The functions and impacts of these emotions vary and are highly context-dependent. For some individuals, the freeze response gives way to a classic fight response: anger; for others, to flight: experiential avoidance. For yet others, it leads to fright: anxiety; and lastly for some, to faint: learned helplessness.

In terms of emotions for clinicians to be aware of, we suggest following the primary emotions as described by Greenberg (2004) in emotion-focused therapy: anger, sadness, disgust/shame, and fear. Secondary emotions may cover the primary and hence confuse the therapist. For example, an individual may present as highly angry, but further exploration may reveal a deep-seated sadness that is being masked by the anger. Furthermore, in accordance with emotionally focused therapy (Brubacher, 2018), we suggest that clinicians consider the role that instrumental emotions play: these are the expressed emotions that have the aim of influencing others. For example, expression of anger which is intended to control others' behaviour in a particular way. These may be present both in the client's personal life and in the therapeutic relationship. We recommend noticing the expressed emotions and their functions in order to unpack which type of emotion is being presented, and how this may be influencing and influence the individual's level of functioning in their day-to-day life.

Cognitive

Assessment of cognitive styles and processes is key to understanding how an individual is consciously making sense of their experiences of loss and their cognitive coping styles. We recommend that clinicians focus on clients' cognitions in relation to the past (rumination), future (worry), present (intrusions, flashbacks), as well as cognitive coping styles (e.g. avoidance). This will enable clinicians to develop a case conceptualisation as presented in Chapter 3.

When assessing the client's cognitive patterns and style, we recommend that clinicians attend to the following:

- Form and mode of thinking style, this could be in response to emotion, body sensation, images, or intrusions
- Content of thoughts (the exact display of thought, if it could be described)
- Cognitive triggers
- Cognitive avoidance
- How the individual perceives and describes their experiences
- Analysis and re-evaluation of their thoughts, self-critical stance, blame and shaming of self

- Negatory thought patterns that are associated with the individual's beliefs about themselves, others, and the world we live in
- Presence of harmful thoughts: content, intent, and plan

It is also important to hold the cognitive specificity hypothesis (Beck, 1976) in mind during this part of the assessment. Beck suggested that psychological difficulties can be differentiated through fine-grained exploration of the automatic thoughts and appraisals an individual makes. Research has shown that depression and anxiety (Beck et al., 1987) as well as various mood states (Beck & Perkins, 2001) can be distinguished using the cognitive specificity hypothesis. We apply the cognitive specificity hypothesis to contexts of loss: we suggest that each prior loss an individual has experienced has a specific set of components that set it apart from other losses and the current loss. Careful questioning can unpick these differences in triggers, emotions, feelings, thoughts, and coping strategies. It may be that the current loss triggers prior losses, and there may be parallel experiences across losses; however, each loss and its experiences are unique to the individual, and hence can be differentiated. For example, the loss of a partner can be differentiated from the loss of a child in terms of core emotions, cognitions, feelings, and behaviours. Perhaps more clearly, these losses can be differentiated based on their meaning and the impact on the individual's functioning. Therefore, each loss context has a specific set of experiences associated with it, and teasing these apart in the assessment process can help both clinicians and clients to better understand the scope and nature of their grieving.

Physical Sensations

Given that grief may be associated with experiences akin to those of obsessive-compulsive disorder or post-traumatic stress disorder, we suggest that clinicians pay close attention to physical sensations which may resemble embodied flashbacks/intrusions. It would be especially pertinent to explore whether certain physical sensations act as triggers for emotive or cognitive manoeuvres, for example: somatic reliving which triggers emotional dysregulation, resulting in cognitive avoidance. This part of the assessment will also require an exploration of physical safety and shelter; individuals who live in an unsafe physical environment or whose basic physical needs (e.g. hunger, thirst, warmth) are not being met require a very different formulation and treatment plan to those whose basic needs are met. Clinicians can enquire about this by asking questions relating to an individual's place of residence and how safe they feel. Information gathered relating to basic physical needs and safety will feature in the longitudinal formulation, as presented in Chapter 3.

Assessing body responses requires an understanding of:

- An increase in tension
- Palpitation, anxiety, or panic symptoms
- Loss of mobility or reduction in movements
- Changes in body sensation including pain and discomfort
- This may be provided in some cultures as an emotional response, such as my heart is aching

There are some key components of information gathered from the assessment that clinicians need to be aware of – especially given the current context of a global pandemic where individuals are increasingly disconnected and isolated from support systems. One major factor to consider is the impact that (lack of) sensory stimulation in social contexts can have on the client. Clinicians are encouraged to gather information on touch, smell, sight, and hearing which may link to the client's current emotional state, how attuned they are with their difficulties, and the sensory needs that may arise as a result.

Behavioural

In terms of behaviours, we suggest that clinicians focus on how clients are managing challenging emotions, cognitions, and physical sensations in relation to loss. It may help clinicians to unpick behavioural responses by focusing on what has changed for the individual since the loss by asking questions that help clients to identify tangible behavioural changes that have occurred as a result of the loss. This may include coping styles such as behavioural avoidance (e.g. social withdrawal) or enactment of emotional distress (e.g. aggressive behaviour towards others, compulsive-like repetition of behaviours). It is useful to explore behaviours that have changed since the loss, as well as any further changes that have occurred over time. In addition to this, we suggest that clinicians assess positive/useful behavioural coping styles which help with emotion regulation and processing of grief. For example, social withdrawal may be a positive coping strategy if an individual's social network is generating shame or guilt in them. Therefore, there are no inherently "pathological" behaviours; each must be assessed in relation to its context and its function for the individual. Making this distinction will help clinicians to better understand which behaviours maintain distress and which ameliorate it.

We recommend that clinicians assess for behavioural responses such as:

- Behaviours in response to triggers
- Changes in behaviours that was not a normal routine for the individual

- Specific behaviours that help the person with their coping
- Overactivity, tasking in order to taxing the memory
- Increase in exercise and preoccupation
- Increased in engaging in discussion; preoccupation
- Seeking response or meaning that could explain
- Increase in ritualistic behaviours
- Increase or decrease in religiosity
- Substance or alcohol misuse, or significant increase
- Harmful behaviours including erratic and usual behaviours

Protective Factors

A matrix assessment is not complete without an understanding of the individual's protective factors. This part of the assessment focuses on all the strengths, resources, and resiliences available to an individual. This may include protective factors which are currently being under-utilised, as well as those that the client is currently employing to help them cope. It is important for the clinician to explore internal (personal skills and strengths) as well as external (social connections, contextual factors) protective factors. This part of the assessment can include an exploration of what the individual has already tried to help them cope, which will illuminate their natural coping styles and existing coping strategies.

In relation to social protective factors, clinicians can explore sexual and romantic relationships, friendships, family relationships, religious and cultural communities, and activity-based communities (e.g. friends from football club). Additionally, we recommend that clinicians unpick social protective factors to deepen understanding of relational factors and values which may feature in the longitudinal formulation (see Chapter 3). This includes asking questions about work/education, the value/importance of this for the individual. It is important to assess how able the person feels to engage with these activities, and what function these activities play (e.g. bringing release from ever-present rumination, creating opportunities for experiencing a sense of achievement, triggering guilt for enjoying work when one is "supposed to be grieving" etc.).

We also suggest that clinicians assess clients' relationship with acceptance at this stage; the more they are able to recognise their values, make compromises, and accept certain elements of their current lived experience, the greater their ability to cope. This exploration of acceptance and coping will support the development of a case conceptualisation, as explored in detail in Chapter 3.

We recommend that clinicians assess for:

- The positive aspects of their life and what has gone well for them
- Their motivation and drive for change, if any
- The person's access to supportive people and social networks

It is important to ensure that protective factors are explored in sufficient depth. For example, if the person says they have friends, the clinician cannot leave it there. They need to ask more: Are your friends compassionate towards you? Are your friends supportive? In what way? What do they do for you? Does that help you? Does that make you feel any better?

Clinical Observations

During the assessment session, we encourage clinicians to be aware of the silent dialogue: that which is not being said. In terms of evolution, there are many emotional experiences that individuals may conceal or avoid discussing, such as fear, shame, guilt, and embarrassment. This may prevent clients from fully engaging with the process. It is the role of the clinician to be attuned to the client's unspoken communications and to consider what might underlie them. This can be facilitated through careful behavioural observations, including noting the client's ability to engage, their appearance, the severity of their emotionality (e.g. seen through body language), their stance towards the loss, and their stance towards supportive/nurturing others.

Specific Assessment

Accounts of Specific Loss-Related Experiences

This part of the assessment focuses on gaining a comprehensive understanding of the impact of the loss on the affective, cognitive, and behavioural experiences of the client. We suggest using CBT approach and techniques that readers will be familiar with in exploring these elements of clients' experiences – however, it is important to ensure that the focus is on the impact of the loss on these elements of functioning, rather than the symptoms themselves.

After orienting oneself to the client's functioning in relation to general daily activities, the next stage of the assessment involves an exploration of the client's specific concerns, as well as the motivations and values underlying those concerns. We recommend beginning this conversation with an open question, as with typical therapeutic approaches, such as "what brings you here today?" – but again, we emphasise the need to focus not on symptomatology, but on underlying motivations. For example, if the client says "I'm unable to cope without the person who died", we can use Socratic questioning to ask what is causing the person to feel unable to cope, unable to move on, unable to exist, unable to live, and so on. For example, by asking "what gives you the impression that you can't cope?", "what elements of your life do you feel unable to cope in?"

The underlying meaning that the individual attributes to their distress is what maintains that distress in the present. The meaning given may be based on a strong emotional experience such as fear, anxiety, confidence, guilt, or shame, or based on familiar rituals or spiritual/religious faith and experiences. For example, a client may report that they did not cry as much at the funeral as other people did and that this makes them a bad person. If the clinician were to approach this from a second-wave CBT approach, they may ask questions relating to the frequency of crying, triggers for crying, and changes in this since the loss. In the approach we outline here, which is embedded in third-wave CBT approaches, we would encourage the clinician to ask questions relating to the meaning that the client makes of this experience. For instance, questions such as: What does crying mean to you? What does it mean about you that you didn't cry as much as others? Is it about "you didn't cry?" or "you shouldn't cry?"?. This line of questioning allows the clinician to consider the cultural and contextual factors which influence the individual's meaning-making processes, and ultimately maintain their presenting distress. Following this exploration of meanings, the clinician can begin to identify the emotional, cognitive, physiological, and behavioural triggers for those meaning-making processes.

The specific assessment allows clinicians to understand the contextual factors and triggers that make the client feel stuck. By unpicking the "stuckness", the clinician can begin to understand the trigger points idiosyncratic to the client. In the example given above, the client may explain that they know they can't cope because the person they lost provided them with emotional support, without which they feel completely at sea. This suggests that supportiveness is valued by the client and that it may be moments that remind them of this loss of support, perhaps moments in which they feel emotionally overwhelmed and can no longer rely on the person whom they have lost – which are trigger points for feelings of stuckness.

When exploring the stuckness, the clinician can ask gentle questions to understand the level of control and choice that the client has in relation to their difficulties – not to begin the change process, but to ascertain the degree of flexibility of thought and the capacity for reflexivity that will be required further in therapeutic intervention. An example line of questioning is as follows: "Do you think you are struggling with your difficulties/with the loss?" – and if the client answers "yes", then we would ask "Do you have any control or choice over that matter?". This helps the clinician to understand what motivates the individual to hold their position and to explore the degree to which they have considered alternative perspectives and conceptualisations of their current difficulties.

The specific assessment intends to unpick not only the coping behaviours and strategies that the client has access to, but the functional impact of those behaviours. Focusing on understanding the function of behaviours is central to this model. In relation to coping strategies, we suggest that clinicians ask specific questions to explore the function that the behaviours serve, as well as the usefulness of coping strategies in the short-, medium-, and long-term. Rather than assuming that we understand the function of a coping behaviour (e.g. based on past experiences of working within the CBT model and with safety behaviours), we suggest that clinicians remain open and curious (Rogers, 1951) to explore the emotional functions of behaviours as well as their unintended consequences (Gilbert, 2010).

The fictitious session script below provides an example of this in action:

THERAPIST: How're you currently coping?
CLIENT: I keep busy.
T: What happens when you do that?
SU: I don't think about it.
T: Does it help?
SU: I'm okay if I'm not thinking about it.
T: What happens when you think about it?

In addition to a focus on the function of coping behaviours, we suggest that clinicians consider individual's ability and capacity to tolerate distress and regulate their emotions. We recommend the use of theory and techniques from dialectical behaviour therapy (DBT; Linehan, 2020), specifically modules focusing on emotion regulation and distress tolerance. According to DBT theorists, there are five types of response to a problem: solving the problem, changing one's emotional response, tolerating the distress, remaining distressed, or exacerbating the distress. In relation to loss, the problem is unsolvable – therefore, individuals seeking therapy may be preferentially using one of the other types of coping, or a mixture of multiple approaches, to manage their distress. Unpicking how the person is responding to the loss – including triggers and their idiosyncratic meanings – can help clinicians to understand how many different types of coping skills the person has access to, which ones they preferentially use, and how useful these skills are in relation to their day-to-day functioning (Feigenbaum, 2019).

Value-Based Assessment

We provide an overview here of a values-based assessment that can be used optionally as part of an extended assessment process. This is based on an exploration of the individual's past, present, and future values in order to aid a then-vs-now-vs-next comparison in relation to the loss. This comparative process adds to pre-existing literature relating to values-based working within an ACT framework (Hayes et al., 2011) and is based on premises of Eye Movement Desensitisation and Reprocessing (EMDR; Shapiro, 2002). EMDR suggests that in order to overcome adversity, we need to be able to reassess past values, the present dilemma or conflict, and to link this to plans for the future.

Using three sheets of paper, we recommend that clinicians identify and explore clients' past, present, and future values. By listing them in this way, we support clients to understand changes in values and to make links with the impact of the loss. Clinicians are recommended to ask about difficulties as well as values in relation to the past, present, and future. This information can be incorporated into the formulation and inform treatment planning. This process aims to support individuals to become gradually aware of the changes that have occurred due to the loss, and the impact of these changes on their identity, experiences, functioning, and coping. It is also intended to feed into the intervention, whereby clinicians can scaffold clients to change, evolve, or develop new values for the future.

In order to do this, we use the three-page exercise outlined earlier. The intention is to create distance between the experience and the self (defusion) and to break down impact into cognitions, feelings, physical body sensations, and behaviours. We can ask clients about how much distance there is between their values and the current situation, and link this to their ways of making sense of the loss. By linking values and meaning-making, we can support clients to understand where the discrepancies lie, and why some discrepancies are causing more distress than others (Park, 2005).

Working with Neurotypical and Neurodiverse Young People

There are many young people who have experienced significant losses in their lives. These losses may be due to death – for example, the loss of parents, grandparents, siblings, pets (e.g. Jarolmen, 1998) – or for other reasons, such as being taken into foster care (Russell, 2002), experiencing migration, anticipating the loss of parent(s) who have terminal illnesses and so on. Whilst the overall principles of the Principles of Loss model can be used with young people, the way the model is applied – especially in relation to assessment and intervention – varies based on the age, developmental stage, and cognitive and social abilities of the individual. This section aims to briefly outline the contexts of loss which young people may find themselves in, and ways in which we can consider tailoring the Principles of Loss model to the needs of children and young people. Although we provide here an overview of working with young people, it is beyond the scope of this book to furnish the reader with a comprehensive account of grief in children. We refer clinicians unfamiliar with grief in children to the following books: Living With Grief: Children, Adolescents and Loss (Doka, 2013), and Grief in Children: A Handbook for Adults Second Edition (Dyregrov, 2008).

When working with young people, it is important to ensure that we conduct a thorough assessment of the social network, previous experiences of loss, and the young person's ability to adapt to change. This also includes assessing for learning and communication difficulties in order to inform the formulation and intervention. The age that the young person accesses services as well as the age at which they experienced the loss are also important factors to consider. Young people aged 12 and upwards at the point of contact with services are more likely to be able to engage in cognitive processing of the loss. On the other hand, children younger than 12 at the point of accessing therapy may require interventions using creative, emotion-led (St Thomas & Johnson, 2007) and storytelling-based approaches (Scaletti & Hocking, 2010) such as narrative, imagery, and arts-based work. We detail this further below.

In this model, we especially focus on the attachment-related impact (Kosminsky & Jordan, 2016) of the loss on the young person's emotional regulation, ability to cope, and daily functioning. It is not only parents who function as attachment objects; any being or object (e.g. transitional objects) which hold specific meaning to the young person can have attachment-related functions. The depth of the attachment, age of the loss (Brack et al., 1993), and the quality of the remaining social network determine the extent of the impact of the loss on the young person. Having better attachment resources (i.e. multiple "good enough" attachment objects) in the context of loss means that the young person is more likely to survive the experience and to lead a better quality of life (Buelow et al., 2002). This is because they are able to draw on their social network in order to have their emotional needs met by other caregivers and important figures in their life, which enables them to process the loss in an adaptive manner. For young people who lack this level of social support and attachment resource, experiencing significant loss early in life can have a traumatic impact on their development and functioning.

Often in grief work, there is a disconnect between emotions and cognitions: individuals may be able to make sense of the loss cognitively, but their emotions remain painful and impair their functionality. Therapy is about working together to find an adaptive emotional response that is proportional to the loss, and facilitates the individual in regaining their lost functionality. In order to do so, the point of acceptance needs to be worked towards; the individual cannot be detached completely from the loss experience (this would be linked with unhelpful avoidance strategies), but they also cannot be completely overwhelmed every time they remember the loss (akin to a hypervigilant trauma response). There is a need to find an adaptive response to the loss which helps the person to navigate their grief and regain functioning. This can be framed in many different ways (e.g. coping strategies, acceptance), but the overarching concept is to hold both a state of rational understanding and emotional ambivalence in the mind at the body at the same time. In order to be able to hold such ambivalence and conflicting emotions and thoughts in mind at once, the individual requires reorientation to their axis of self – the anchor which holds them in place whilst they navigate the turbulence of the loss. Following loss, the axis of self may be misaligned – as in the above example, where there is cognitive understanding without emotional catharsis. The greater this misalignment between cognition and emotion, the greater the distress.

When working with young people, it is likely that the axis of self is itself still-forming or newly formed. The axis of self is not yet strong enough or defined enough to act as an anchor during turbulence. Therefore, the young person may experience heightened distress in relation to identity and selfhood in the aftermath of loss – for example, asking questions of themselves and others such as "who am I?" and "what is my purpose?". Loss can destabilise the whole system and axis of self, which means that the young person must not only rediscover their identity but may even need to rebuild that identity from scratch as a result. Therefore, grief work with CYP focuses more on identity and selfhood than it may with adults.

Working with Children of Different Ages

Regardless of the child or young person's age, the first step to a comprehensive assessment involves examining their cognitive and adaptive skills. The developmental and cognitive abilities of the young person will determine to a large extent the nature of the intervention, and this must be a priority for clinicians wishing to tailor their approach for working with children. The following subsection refers to children who do not present with learning disabilities or neurodiversities.

Children may experience loss at a very young age. For example, those who lose an attachment figure in the first two years of life (Norris-Shortle et al., 1993) have very different emotional needs in comparison to a child who loses an attachment figure at the age of 10. In the case of an infant, the priority is to find them an attachment figure to replace the one they have lost. This is likely to come from their existing social network, and so the therapeutic work is likely to involve both caregivers and the infant using parenting-informed approaches.

Toddlers and young children aged 3 to 9 are likely to present with externalising behaviours such as crying and bursts of anger. Children of this age require support in down-regulating these painful emotions and up-regulating pleasurable emotions in the aftermath of loss. Clinical intervention is likely to include a mixture of storytelling (Scaletti & Hocking, 2010), play-based work, and imaginal rescripting – involving the development of a positive state of compassion towards the self, as well as scripting a new future. When working with children under the age of 9, a developmental lens must be used. It is recommended that the clinician uses an emotion-focused, play- or arts-based storytelling approach that does not require active cognitive processing.

Children aged 9 to 12 are likely to require a mixture of creative and play-based approaches, and cognitive processing of the loss. Children who are aged 12 and above are developmentally more able to have cognitive and rational conversations with adults. They are capable of engaging with a more cognitive style of questioning and intervention. However, this must always be done within the context of attachment, and with a strong emphasis on the young person's emotional experiences. It is likely that children and young people aged 12 and up will require support in developing the axis of self and an adaptive self-identity.

Working with Neurodiversity

When working with neurodiverse children it is important to spend ample time during the assessment phase to better understand the young person's needs and any adjustments that may be required in the therapeutic approach. In this section we focus especially on children and young people with a diagnosis of autism, although these concepts can also be applied to children with learning disabilities, and other neurodiverse experiences.

A step-by-step approach is needed when working with neurodiverse children, and particular care is taken to ensure that the pace of the therapeutic work matches their cognitive and emotional needs. The first stage of intervention involves gradually introducing the young person to strategies to manage and stabilise their emotions, and to begin introducing change in a staggered manner. We suggest that clinicians spend a significant amount of time in developing a strong therapeutic relationship with the young person, perhaps focusing on their areas of interest or using creative approaches to create a safe space for the young person to express themselves freely. It may be useful to speak with caregivers alongside this process in order to gather further information about the nature of the loss and the extent of the impact of the loss on the young person. This reduces the cognitive burden placed on the child and provides contextual information for the clinician to begin generating hypotheses and formulating the difficulties that the young person may be experiencing. It also ensures that the clinician can devote time to develop a strong trusting therapeutic relationship without needing to pressure the young person to talk about the loss straight away. This parallel process can also be containing for caregivers and support them in developing their own skills in emotion regulation, and hence facilitate their ability to role model and scaffold the young person's emotional development.

If the young person used to have a nurturing and supportive relationship with the person who has been lost (e.g. a parent, sibling, teacher, support worker, etc.), they may not be able to tolerate the degree of threat posed by this change. For some young people, a transitional object may be needed to support their capacity to self-soothe and to reduce the intensity of the loss. Attachment in the context of neurodiversity is especially important to consider. The inclusion of an attachment figure in the aftermath of loss is likely to support the young person by minimising the amount of additional change they must navigate. This may mean meeting with both caregiver and young person together to reinforce the relationship between them and increase moments of connection and nurture. As clinicians, we can scaffold adults to provide a "good enough" secure base for the young person in sessions, to support them in doing this more consistently in the young person's day-to-day life. This can increase empathy in the social system, and hence improve functional outcomes for the CYP. If the person who was lost was the primary attachment figure, it may be necessary to begin working with other adults in the network who can "replace" the lost object. This may mean understanding who the next-best person would be to act as an attachment figure for the young person. It is especially important, particularly in the context of social care, to consider that this "new" primary attachment figure needs to be consistently available and not at threat of being lost themselves (i.e. not a transient figure such as a temporary support worker).

When working with children with autism, we recommend that clinicians assess for signs of increased distress, which may present as an increase in unhelpful behaviours, increased repetitive movements, introduction of new ritualistic behaviours, or introduction of new specific interests. It is important to notice these changes, and to address them as early as possible as they can become habitual or entrenched over time, and maybe more difficult to address after a lot of time has passed. Caregivers and others in the social network can be helpful informants in relation to these behavioural changes across contexts (e.g. at home, in school, during day care). In assessment and intervention with CYP with autism, we recommend having shorter conversations relating to emotional distress, especially in the early stages where focus on the therapeutic relationship takes priority. We also note that CYP with autism may be good at compartmentalising information such that they can comprehend more cognitive or "rational" information more easily than emotion-based information. This may mean that clinicians focus on presenting information cognitively and coherently to begin with, in order to work with emotions in a structured way later on in the therapy. We also highlight the need to adjust our language in line with the young person's needs and communication skills. Asking open-ended emotion-focused questions such as "how are you feeling?" are likely to be experienced as bewildering or uncontaining. Instead, we suggest the use of closed or concrete questions, and taking a more practical/behaviour-based approach to questioning for example "what did you do today? Have you eaten?"

Summary

The assessment is a progressive process of gathering information and developing our ideas in an iterative and collaborative manner, reiterated in order for the client and the clinician become more aware and attuned to the reported difficulties. In order to develop a clear understanding of the presenting problem, collaboration and trust play a great role – as with any other mode of therapeutic intervention. There are a number of key factors to be considered during the assessment phase, notably a clear understanding of the developmental and progression of difficulties in line with changes and losses throughout the individual's life up to the present day.

As clinicians, we conduct a thorough mental health assessment as part of a typical therapeutic process; the specific assessment is simply an expansion of that with a more refined focus on loss, functionality, and meaning-making. The specific assessment offers a greater and more detailed understanding of the process leading to the loss, previous losses and their impact, and the individual's ability to cope with previous and current loss/es. In some instances, the actual loss/es are catalysts to other distressing ways of meaning-making. In other cases, there may be a sense of relief, although the reflection and intrusions of the experience could still be troublesome. Assessing the specific content in this fine-grained manner enables better awareness of the state of mind; such as emotional triggers, meaning attached to the experienced emotional exposures and individual feelings about the experiences reported.

As a part of the specific assessment, we encourage the client to provide a narrative of their experiences; they're telling us the story of their losses. The assessment extracts information linked to those losses and how the person has been able to recover or not. Many people feel frozen in time ("I can't move on" "I don't know how to move on") and feel stuck there for a long time. The aim of the assessment is to answer the question: What makes it different with this loss that makes the person get stuck?

We recommend that clinicians focus on external and internal emotive triggers. The emotional triggers could be a range of factors relating to different senses (sight, hearing, touch), and internal memory recall. Both these types of triggers provide the electrical impulses for the person to think about their loss. Following this, a cognitive value/meaning is added to that emotional trigger and experience, which then provides the subsequent feeling. These differences in meaning-making explain individual differences in navigating loss. For example, when looking at a photo of loved one who was lost, if the meaning is positive (e.g. "we had such a wonderful time on that holiday together"), it would trigger a pleasant feeling. On the other hand, if the meaning is negative (e.g. "I'll never have a holiday as good as that one again, because we won't be together"), it triggers a negative feeling. The assessment aims to extract this information – what are the patterns, the common themes across losses? Is the individual more likely to be triggered by visual cues? By sensory cues? By internal cues (memory recall)? Understanding the client's experiences to this level of detail creates a reference point for both therapist and client, which forms the basis of the formulation and treatment plan.

References

Beck, A. T. (1976). *Cognitive therapy and the emotional disorders*. New American Freedom.

Beck, A. T., Brown, G., Steer, R. A., Eidelson, J. I., & Riskind, J. H. (1987). Differentiating anxiety and depression: A test of the cognitive content-specificity hypothesis. *Journal of Abnormal Psychology*, 96(3), 179.

Beck, R., & Perkins, T. S. (2001). Cognitive content-specificity for anxiety and depression: A meta-analysis. *Cognitive Therapy and Research*, 25(6), 651–663.

Bracha, H. S. (2004). Freeze, flight, fight, fright, faint: Adaptationist perspectives on the acute stress response spectrum. *CNS Spectrums*, 9(9), 679–685.

Brack, G., Gay, M. F., & Matheny, K. B. (1993). Relationships between attachment and coping resources among late adolescents. *Journal of College Student Development*, 34(3), 212–215.

Brubacher, L. L. (2018). *Stepping into emotionally focused couple therapy: Key ingredients of change*. Routledge.

Buelow, S. A., Lyddon, W. J., & Johnson, J. T. (2002). Client attachment and coping resources. *Counselling Psychology Quarterly*, 15(2), 145–152.

Doka, K. J. (2013). *Living with grief: Children, adolescents and loss*. Routledge.

Dyregrov, A. (2008). *Grief in children: A handbook for adults second edition*. Jessica Kingsley.

Feigenbaum, J. (2019). *Dialectical behaviour therapy* [lecture]. University College London.

Gilbert, P. (2010). *The compassionate mind: A new approach to life's challenges*. Constable.

Greenberg, L. S. (2004). Emotion-focused therapy. *Clinical Psychology & Psychotherapy: An International Journal of Theory & Practice*, 11(1), 3–16.

Hayes, S. C., Strosahl, K. D., & Wilson, K. G. (2011). *Acceptance and commitment therapy: The process and practice of mindful change*. Guilford Press.

Jarolmen, J. (1998). A comparison of the grief reaction of children and adults: Focusing on pet loss and bereavement. *OMEGA-Journal of Death and Dying*, 37(2), 133–150.

Kosminsky, P. S., & Jordan, J. R. (2016). *Attachment-informed grief therapy: The clinician's guide to foundations and applications*. Routledge.

Linehan, M. M. (2020). *Dialectical behavior therapy in clinical practice*. Guilford Publications.

Macneil, C. A., Hasty, M. K., Conus, P., & Berk, M. (2012). Is diagnosis enough to guide interventions in mental health? Using case formulation in clinical practice. *BMC medicine*, 10(1), 1–3.

Norris-Shortle, C., Young, P. A., & Williams, M. A. (1993). Understanding death and grief for children three and younger. *Social Work*, 38(6), 736–742.

Park, C. L. (2005). Religion as a meaning-making framework in coping with life stress. *Journal of Social Issues*, 61(4), 707–729.

Pearlman, L. A., Wortman, C. B., Feuer, C. A., Farber, C. H., & Rando, T. A. (2014). *Treating traumatic bereavement: A practitioner's guide*. Guilford Publications.

Rogers, C. R. (1951). *Client centred therapy: Its current practice, implications and theory constable.* Houghton Mifflin.

Russell, P. L. (2002). *Attachment and grief in foster children*. Alliant International University, San Francisco Bay.

Scaletti, R., & Hocking, C. (2010). Healing through story telling: An integrated approach for children experiencing grief and loss. *New Zealand Journal of Occupational Therapy, 57*(2), 66–71.

Shapiro, F. (2002). EMDR treatment: Overview and integration. In F. Shapiro (Ed.), *EMDR as an integrative psychotherapy approach: Experts of diverse orientations explore the paradigm prism* (pp. 27–55). American Psychological Association. https://doi.org/10.1037/10512-002

St Thomas, B., & Johnson, P. (2007). *Empowering children through art and expression: Culturally sensitive ways of healing trauma and grief*. Jessica Kingsley.

Watkins, A. (2015). *Why You Feel What You Feel*. YouTube. www.youtube.com/watch?v=h-rRgpPbR5w.

Chapter 3

Formulation and Case Conceptualisation

Overview

Following a comprehensive assessment, the next stage is formulation and case conceptualisation. This is a process that readers will be familiar with, as it is a common component in CBT and third-wave therapeutic interventions. Whilst we base our formulation and case conceptualisation on the basics from second- and third-wave CBT approaches, we also provide novel components tailored to the model outlined in Chapter 1, based on the needs of individuals who have experienced loss. The data from the Loss and Grief Functionality Questionnaire (LAG-FQ) need to be integrated with additional information gathered in the generic and specific parts of the assessment. The clinician needs to develop an understanding of how the client managed previous losses, how their lived experiences (e.g. coming from a war zone) impact them, and what it is about this particular loss that has created such a significant impact on them.

When an individual experiences a loss, there is a need to acculturate (Ward, 1996) to it in order to assimilate the emotional- and meaning-related impact on the self. Loss by definition is a problem without a solution; suffering and grief arise when the individual realises (perhaps not at a conscious level) that problem cannot be solved. For example, if you lost your mobile phone, the first step would be to solve the problem by searching for the phone. If the phone cannot be found, you may begin to experience annoyance, frustration, worry, and so on. Suffering in the face of loss consists of two parts: the inability to solve the problem, and coming to terms with this. If the problem is easily solved, there would be no suffering; suffering only occurs when the individual continues to search for a solution to an unsolvable problem, resulting eventually in a series of symptoms associated with that suffering (e.g. worry, rumination, low mood, etc.). There are many contributing factors to this process that shape the nature and extent of the suffering that an individual experiences, for example: early life relational patterns, predispositions to perfectionism, understandings of "right" and "wrong", ability to problem-solve, coping skills,

DOI: 10.4324/9781003214045-3

degree of self-reflection – awareness and recognition of own limitations, and ability to accept change.

We can predict that an individual with strong moral beliefs regarding right and wrong, who has a greater tendency to perfectionism, may struggle more to cope with loss due to their preference for finding a solution than someone else who might have a greater preference for acceptance and has the coping skills required to do so. However, we must not assume that if an individual seems to more readily accept their loss, they are not suffering – the acceptance may be partial in nature, spoken of cognitively without the associated emotional acceptance.

Developing a formulation based on these longitudinal and dispositional factors helps us to better understand a person's suffering, its development and maintenance, as well as possible next steps for therapeutic intervention. There are three main outcomes to unsuccessful problem-solving in the face of loss: problem-solving (freeze response), learned helplessness (flight response), or heightened distress (fight response). The initial response to loss is likely to be "freeze" as the individual attempts to solve the problem. If they come to understand that the problem cannot be solved, they may move into a state of fight – characterised by anger, frustration, blame, and unfairness, or into a state of flight – characterised by learned helplessness, low mood, apathy, and demotivation. In some individuals, there may be a state of partial acceptance, whereby they have consciously accepted that there is no solution to the loss, but continue to attempt to problem-solve in the back of the mind – namely ruminating on the loss. Therefore, partial acceptance does not necessitate a lack of suffering.

Developing a formulation involves exploring the current narrative of the person's circumstances, providing a positive nurturing role that supports the individual to recount the loss, containing distressing cognitions, and validating the emotions. The role of the assessment and formulation is to develop an understanding of the triggers, their frequency and impact, as well as facilitating the client's ability to reflect on their current circumstances in a safe and non-judgemental manner. Attempting to do more at this stage would be counterproductive to the development of a strong and trusting therapeutic relationship. During formulation, the clinician is attempting to understand the client's contexts, help them to feel heard in their suffering, and to validate their compassion and self-soothing skills.

We warn clinicians against conflating self-compassion and self-pity, as these are different processes with disparate functions. A nurturing self-soothing self-compassionate stance is rooted in compassion-focused therapy principles relating to the acknowledgement of pain, and the taking of responsibility to alleviate that pain. However, self-pity is a communicative stance that aims to demonstrate to others the extent of the suffering and to highlight that the individual feels alone and unsupported by others. Self-pity is an example of partial compassion, whereby they recognise their own suffering but seek others to take responsibility for alleviating this. This demonstrates the individual's (implicit) understanding of their own limitations in coping and soothing skills, and hence plays the function of seeking the support from others that they feel unable to provide for themselves. Self-pity is therefore a help-seeking communication and is not a negative thing – crucially, self-pity is an adaptive response based on a recognition of one's own limitations. In such situations, the clinician's role is twofold: they need to provide compassion as to do otherwise would be experienced as unempathetic and unkind, and they need to educate the client about suffering and compassion to scaffold development of self-soothing skills in the longer term.

By developing an understanding of the contexts that a client comes from and returns to, allows the clinician to adapt their stance accordingly. Different clients seek different things from therapy; some may need to address the loss directly, others to explore their self-identity in relation to the loss, some may seek support in navigating cultural practices relating to loss, and others may need to resolve conflicts between differing elements of self-identity. In the process of formulation, the clinician begins to develop an understanding of the client's needs, and what they may be seeking from therapy.

For example, a client may present with an absence of joy due to an inability to find a solution to the problem of loss; they may have a primary cognitive drive to solve the presented problem and gain a positive feeling from that resolution. Grief in this instance is formulated as a process whereby the problem-solving skills have become the stuck point. The individual remains in a state of limbo, attempting and re-attempting to solve an unsolvable problem, and becoming increasingly frustrated with themselves and others who are unable to help them with this. In this scenario, the client is left with two choices: to persist in seeking a solution ("Why has this happened to me?"), or to accept the fragility of life as a first step towards processing the loss (i.e. to accept the outcome).

Longitudinal and Contextual Formulation

The reader will be familiar with the utility of formulation in establishing the impact of the different features of a client's experiences on their current life, and the use of formulation to understand the development and maintenance of current distress. We use some elements of the manualised treatment of traumatic grief developed by Pearlman et al. (2014), with additional components grounded in our own theoretical and clinical model to support readers in working clinically with loss. Pearlman et al. (2014) conceptualise formulation as: an understanding of the context of the loss, the nature and meaning made of this loss, the client's responses to loss, changes in their life since the loss, the relationship between the client and the lost object, their self-assessment of coping ability, and the individual's understanding and expectations of the mourning process. Whilst many elements of this overlap with our own conceptualisation, we present below a novel framework for formulating loss based on the 5Ps framework (Macneil et al., 2012).

When completing the formulation, we recommend that clinicians bring together all of the factors that have a significant impact on the individual's current levels of functioning. Following this, the client rates each factor on a scale of 0 to 10 in terms of impact ("How much on a scale of 0–10 does this factor affect your current life, with 0 being 'not at all', and 10 being 'very much'?"). The aim of this task is to help the client and the clinician to understand the differing degrees to which various factors affect the individual, and to begin prioritising factors in order to develop treatment goals that are meaningful and impactful for the client. We also recommend that the clinician combines these scores to create a composite impact score, which can be used to track progression throughout treatment.

Predisposing

As in a typical formulation, we expect this section to include information on the following: early childhood experiences, attachment style, interpersonal dynamics including abandonment or difficult relationships, loss or traumatic loss/es, and exposure to disasters.

Precipitating

This section of the formulation considers various factors that may have contributed to the onset of the current presenting difficulties in relation to the loss, including social, cognitive, emotional, and physical health contexts.

Perpetuating

Clinicians are encouraged to consider specific factors which perpetuate the client's current difficulties, including intrusions, loss-specific triggers (e.g. a name), social contexts (e.g. specific people), and environmental stimuli such as the home or other locations associated with the lost object or the event of the loss itself.

Protective Factors

Exploration of people, places, and behaviours that support the individual in coping is incredibly important. This may include activities such as visiting the grave, talking to the deceased, or symbolic representations and/or rituals based on cultural and/or religious practices.

Current Place of Residence

Loss is often accompanied by significant changes to an individual's physical means and safeties, hence a thorough assessment of the client's current home context is tantamount. Clinicians are encouraged to ask specific questions relating to the individual's living arrangement and sense of security in the aftermath of the loss.

Religiosity and Its Impact

The formulation needs to include an understanding of the client's relationship to religion and/or spirituality, their links to religious communities and spaces, as well as their access to and relationship with religious leaders. As religion is often a taboo topic that many clients feel reticent to broach, we recommend that clinicians explicitly ask about religious faith, and take the lead in opening up this conversation. It is also important to ask deeper questions about the meanings that the individual makes in relation to religion and loss, as there may be instances in which religion is experienced as having a negative connotation, meaning, or impact on the individual's ability to cope with the loss.

Culture and Customs

An in-depth exploration of the client's current cultural practices and customs associated with loss is required. Both positive and negative meanings associated with culture and customs, as well as positive and negative impacts of these on the individual are to be explored. It is also important to gather an understanding of the symbols and rituals associated with loss within the client's cultural context.

Coping

The formulation requires an inclusion of the client's individual skills as well as the skills they can draw on from their social support network in coping with losses – including what worked well in previous experiences of loss, and the strategies currently at their disposal. Exploration of coping can include unpicking the role that rituals play, previous and current ways of coping, as well as the individual's capacity to develop new coping styles (e.g. through social connections). This helps clinicians to better understand the client's coping styles, strategies, degree of functioning, and capacity for positive growth.

Social and Relational Factors

We recommend that clinicians explore the client's current social network to understand who is supportive and who is available or could be accessed should a need arise. It is also important to consider exploring individuals whom the client wishes to avoid or distance themselves from.

Economic Power and Its Impact

Given that loss can have a substantial impact on the financial resources and economic power within a social network, the formulation must consider these factors in order to holistically conceptualise the client's current levels of functioning. Clinicians are encouraged to enquire about the client's financial ability or burden, and the direct/indirect impact of the loss on this.

Work/Education

As with financial impact and economic power, an individual's work/education may be significantly impacted by an experience of loss. It is important for clinicians to consider whether the client is currently active with their work/education, and are able to maintain their position or perform as they wish to do so.

Case Conceptualisation: Here-and-Now Meaning-Making

Overview

Based on the information gathered in the assessment, and integrated in the formulation, we want to make sense of the individual's current difficulties and to begin planning next steps. The process of case conceptualisation involves encouraging the client to become aware of their difficulties, and the patterns that link the past to the present – this is the first step of the treatment. We suggest that clinicians begin the process of case conceptualisation by validating clients' experiences and showing compassion for their pain. Doing so aims to increase the client's window of tolerance, creating a safe space for them to begin making links between different elements of their experience which may be maintaining distress in the here-and-now. Discussions of the past, present, and future need to be had before we move onto speaking about change and compassion; however, clinicians can model compassion from the very beginning of the assessment/formulation stages of treatment in order that clients can internalise and utilise this later in therapy. These initial discussions can be informed by the LAG-FQ, making links between different elements of individuals' experiences and helping them to explore how the loss is affecting them now, as well as their anticipations for the future – what life will be like without the loss.

In developing a case conceptualisation, it is important to ascertain the severity of the change, the impact on the person's life, and the ways in which impairments are being perpetuated in the here-and-now. The change is multifaceted and requires a thorough exploration of various areas of life and functioning, as encompassed by the LAG-FQ. Additionally, the individual's current coping skills and strategies need to be assessed; these can be either positive or negative dependent on their level of functionality, contentment, and ability to return to their previous ways of living. We understand that coping approaches may inadvertently function to maintain the individual's distress at times.

As previously indicated, we firstly need to frame loss as change, evaluate the type and degree of change that has occurred, and how this change is impacting the individual's functioning. It is also relevant to enquire about the person's ability to cope with change and the specific strategies they are using or have used previously. If the individual has experienced losses previously, that might make them more able or more vulnerable in the current loss context – depending on the meaning they made of previous losses and their coping approaches. The previous coping strategies that an individual utilised may have had a positive or negative impact on their recovery. During assessment and formulation, clinicians can explore whether the client is utilising the same or novel coping strategies in comparison to previous experiences of change. This can provide an indication of what works, what is less useful, and the individual's cognitive and behavioural flexibility in the development and adoption of novel and creative strategies for coping.

Psychoeducation

It is important to socialise clients to the model being used, and to explain the rationale for assessment, formulation, and treatment clearly. This helps clients to feel more in control of the process of therapy, increasing agency and hence engagement. It also builds an open and trusting therapeutic relationship, which is key for working with highly painful experiences such as loss. Psychoeducation must be tailored to the individual's needs and experiences; therefore, we suggest that clinicians gather information first (assessment) prior to providing psychoeducation and developing a joint formulation.

The first stage of psychoeducation involves explaining the evolutionary approach taken here, with an explicit focus on the protective system, compassion, and why it's important for us as human beings to help ourselves to solve our own problems. We believe that it is important to note that by definition, coming to therapy is an attempt to solve the problem and that in order to deal with the problem, we have to understand its extent and severity. This requires us as clinicians to give permission for the client to acknowledge their own emotions and the time that it takes to process them; this enables clients to give themselves permission to go through the process of grieving rather than holding themselves to unrealistic standards imposed by society (e.g. "time heals all wounds"). It is important to frame the protective system as something which helps us to deal with the problem (loss), and then to explore the content and function of emotions (distress) and cognitions (rumination, worry, intrusions). This ensures that clients do not feel blamed or pathologised for their grief, and further strengthens the safety and trust in the therapeutic relationship.

Psychoeducation can highlight the fact that intrusive thoughts are evolutionary methods for problem-solving – the brain is trying to solve the problem, to process what has happened – so the brain tries to maintain the problem until it is resolved. This is a protective mechanism that the brain engages in, but has the unintended consequence of maintaining the problem – precisely because death is not a "problem" which can be "solved". Often, the best solution that our minds can find is to shift attention to another task – to keep busy – to keep the conscious cognitive mind occupied in order to prevent the mind from ruminating or worrying (to solve the problem). This is a form of coping which can be a useful strategy for some people. For others it may maintain the difficulty as avoidance perpetuates their distress. Presenting both the possible benefits and drawbacks of coping styles/strategies helps clients to see the protective and detrimental effects inherent in these processes, and enables them to speak more openly about potential strategies they may be using which are not useful to them in the long term.

The next step of psychoeducation needs to focus on the experience of loss itself, with a focus on how this may be felt as a shock – a state of being frozen in time. This links to our protective system and can be associated with fear, avoidance, guilt, shame, and embarrassment. The emotions that are evoked are dependent on the circumstances of the loss – for example, when a life is ended through suicide, the individual may be left with a sense of shame or a sense of regret; in other contexts such as death following prolonged illness, the individual may be left with a sense of acceptance. As clinicians, it is important to name and explain these different possible experiences of loss early in the process; this opens up the space for clients to notice, acknowledge, and explore potentially value-discordant emotions such as disgust, shame, and relief which cannot typically be discussed in social settings.

Here-and-Now Case Conceptualisation

Following basic psychoeducation about the theoretical model, we suggest that clinicians introduce the here-and-now diagram (see Figure 3.1). We recommend that the diagram is introduced to clients in three stages: stage

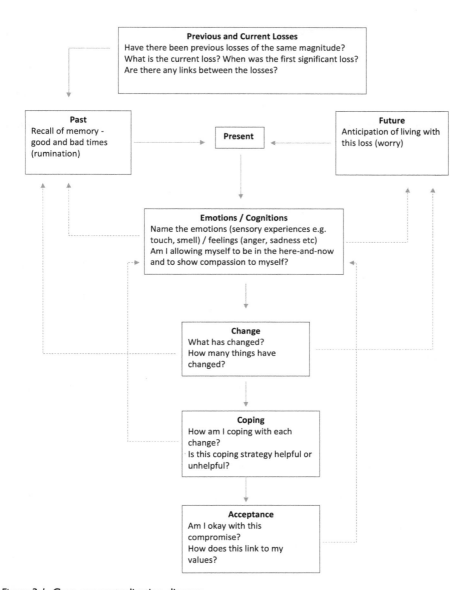

Figure 3.1 Case conceptualisation diagram.

1: past and future, stage 2: present, and stage 3: coping and acceptance. The separation of the formulation into three stages is a protective man-oeuvre; presenting the whole diagram at the start may be overwhelming for clients who have not considered their experience(s) of loss in this way before. By slowly introducing each stage of the formulation, we create a sense of safety and help clients to gradually increase their window of tolerance to accommodate the processing of distressing emotions and experiences. Therefore, case conceptualisation begins with stage 1: consideration of previous and current losses, the past, and the future (see the top section of diagram). After this section has been explored in detail, the next stage can be introduced: present emotions/cognitions, and change. Finally, the last stage is introduced: coping and acceptance. This process may take multiple therapeutic sessions, the pacing of which is led by the client. It is important not to move too quickly through these stages as they can be overwhelming; it is also important not to move too slowly through them as this too risks disengagement from the client.

Working with Young People

Following assessment, the clinician is likely to have a comprehensive overview of the young person's experiences of loss and factors that are helpful and unhelpful in navigating their grief. The formulation stage of therapy is aimed to further explore the positive and negative impacts on the young person and to scaffold their understanding of the ways in which the loss is affecting them intrapsychically and interpersonally.

The formulation of a young person's difficulties focuses on various personal and interpersonal factors. Personal factors include the young person's age and prior experiences of loss, distressing events, or exposure to catastrophes such as war. The formulation also includes a detailed overview of the young person's neurodevelopmental presentation, including their current degree of functionality in relation to the identification, expression, and regulation of emotions, their cognitive abilities, and coping strategies. Relationally, the formulation includes information about the young person's social networks across contexts (e.g. home, school, social clubs, etc.), and in particular there is a need to explore the nature of their relationships – who is experienced as nurturing, who is experienced as emotionally attuned, who is unhelpful, and so on. Gaining a thorough understanding of the young person's access to support, resources (practical and emotional), and the availability of safe and nurturing adults is key.

We can conceptualise a continuum whereby the young person is on one side, and the loss is on the other. Asking the individual to identify what factors (both internal, external, and relational experiences) are positive (closer to them), negative (closer to the loss), and neutral can help both therapist and client to understand the impact of each factor on the person. One way to do this is to put the person in the middle, and write down the positives, negatives, and neutral on a sheet of paper. It may be useful to employ metaphor here – for example, explaining navigating loss as going to war with the bad feelings about losing someone – Who/What are your allies? Who/What are your enemies? Who/What is neutral? This can help the clinician to better understand how the young person is operating and understanding their situation.

Use of visual aids can make a complex process more concrete and clear. It can also provide a clear visual guide for facilitating the young person's understanding about factors in their life that are helpful (and therefore may be increased) and unhelpful (and therefore may need to be decreased) through therapy. In the intervention stage of therapy, this can be revisited to explore what the goals of treatment may be. For example, we can ask young people to consider how many of the negative factors can be dealt with immediately? Which ones can be postponed or resolved later on? This can help to organise the various factors based on their impact on daily functioning, and hence inform treatment goals and processes.

Summary

This chapter has aimed to offer a relational presentation of the difficulties that individuals experiencing loss may face. When collaborating with client, this needs to be simplified to ensure that clients are able to understand the cause and effect of the identified problems and consider the targets to work on in therapy. This involves supporting clients to identify and prioritise the difficulties they're experiencing and develop goals in line with each.

This process will not be too different from an assessment, where we develop a list of difficulties and the relationships between them. In formulation, the clinician focuses on refining this list by identifying their priorities for therapy. The most important part of this process is for clients to get a clearer sense of the triggers, current difficulties, and their goals. This provides the direction for treatment, helps to strengthen the therapeutic alliance, and can buffer against therapeutic drift by setting up a clear expectation of process and outcome for both client and therapist. The client's understanding is of utmost importance, as without this, the therapy cannot proceed. If the client is struggling to conceptualise their loss and grief within this model, we suggest slowing down the pace of the therapy and taking time to gently and slowly explore the formulation with them. We recommend keeping focus on the impact of the loss on the individual, their responses, and how this affects their day-to-day living.

References

Macneil, C. A., Hasty, M. K., Conus, P., & Berk, M. (2012). Is diagnosis enough to guide interventions in mental health? Using case formulation in clinical practice. *BMC Medicine*, *10*(1), 1–3.

Pearlman, L. A., Wortman, C. B., Feuer, C. A., Farber, C. H., & Rando, T. A. (2014). *Treating traumatic bereavement: A practitioner's guide*. Guilford Publications.

Ward, C. (1996). Acculturation. In D. Landis & R. S. Bhagat (Eds.), *Handbook of intercultural training* (pp. 124–147). Sage Publications.

Chapter 4

Intervention

Five-Phase Principles for the Treatment of Loss

The initial focus of therapy is to provide an opportunity for clients to share their narrative and to develop a shared understanding through assessment and formulation. Following assessment, formulation, and case conceptualisation, we envisage that both therapist and client would have a clearer sense of the reported loss or losses, current state of difficulties (including information from the Loss and Grief Functionality Questionnaire [LAG-FQ]), and an increased awareness and understanding of how the individual's previous experiences of loss interact with the current loss and grief.

In this chapter we intend to provide a detailed account of the intervention to be undertaken with clients who are experiencing loss and grief. In addition, there are specific sets of enquiries that clinicians need to bear in mind before engaging with the treatment plan, as indicated below.

This is not a passive approach; it's a proactive approach. Within this model, grief and the cycle of grief are a part of the whole picture – encompassed within the Principles of Loss. The cycle of grief is a by-product of the inability to solve the problem. As humans we try to solve the problem to succeed. When we can't solve the problem, we loop over back to the problem each time we get stuck. This continues until the person comes to the understanding that they are looping over and that this isn't a problem that can be solved in this way. As previously identified, we've taken an evolutionary perspective. And based on that, we need to be able to understand the meaning of loss, the process of experiencing that loss, and how that comes to some form of a resolution. In other words, we are not taking a position of being passive with regards to the experience of loss, grief, and bereavement.

We intend to have a proactive approach in understanding and finding the best resolution for that experience. As an example, we intend to reframe the meaning of loss, grief, and bereavement which we previously alluded to in the theoretical section. In doing so, it is clear that emotional distress is part of that process, therefore understanding the cycle of grief as it has

DOI: 10.4324/9781003214045-4

previously been described by others provides a part of that experience. We understand that the cycle of grief is a by-product of the individual's inability to solve the problem. And as humans, our primary goal is to solve problems and therefore succeed. This is not only an emotional engagement with the problem but an evolutionary perspective. We focus on the meaning that is attached to the loss, and how the process of loss takes place, rather than going over the same emotions within a cyclical pattern.

With the exception of cognitive behavioural therapy (CBT) for bereavement, the majority of models are based on the idea of time as a healer. Although the CBT approach offers a proactive approach, it doesn't consider the client's readiness nor does it focus on functional impact. Our model would enable the person to proactively approach the problem from a functional perspective rooted in evolutionary mechanisms of protection and survival. Previous models of grief provide comprehensive explanations of emotions such as anger and blame – which in our model is linked to a learned helplessness that mimics depression. However, prior models fail to account for other elements of the loss experience such as guilt (as opposed to shame) and disgust.

We also focus here on primary feelings which may underlie the superficial presenting feelings (e.g. zoom in on the sadness underlying anger, rather than on the anger itself) – which is another way in which our model is disparate from prior conceptualisations of loss and grief. These primary feelings are intrinsically linked to our deeper motives and desires and hence create conflicts in the context of loss – the conflict between choice and control, between desire and social restrictions. Secondary emotions arise due to these conflicts, and these secondary emotions are socially constructed and learned responses. For example, a person may feel disgusted with themselves following the loss, but they cannot express this as it would contradict social norms about "acceptable" emotions in the aftermath of loss. Therefore, they may present with sadness or anger (secondary emotions) in order to meet the social needs, whilst subjugating their own emotional needs. This is a point of inner conflict that compounds their distress and hence makes the process of grieving more nuanced. Therefore we suggest looking deeper than the emotions in the cycle of grief, and unpicking the primary feeling that underlies the person's presentation – which will be based on socio-cultural norms and rules, the person's prior experiences of loss and emotion regulation, and their subjective experience of the conflict between choice and control.

Session Structure and Format

The LAG-FQ scoring is scored on a scale of 0–4 for each of the dimensions (change, metacognitive awareness, coping, and acceptance) for each of the 13 items. Each of these dimensions yields a sub-score out of 52.

Table 4.1 LAG-FQ scoring – Sub-scores

Dimension	Score (Each out of 52)
Change	
Metacognitive awareness	
Coping	
Acceptance	
Total score (sum of all of the above)	

Table 4.2 LAG-FQ scoring – Cut-offs

Total Functionality

Degree of functionality	Range of total scores	Recommended number of therapy sessions
Low	0–52	25+
Moderate	53–104	20
Moderately high	105–156	16
High	157–208	10–12

The overall highest possible score is 208, and the lowest overall possible score is 0. The lower the score, the lower the functionality; the higher the score, the higher the functionality. Overall scores below 52 indicate that the person is not functioning well. Anything above 52 suggests that there is at least some partial functioning, but to varying degrees.

The sub-scales can be scored separately to help clients and therapists understand areas that may require more or less focus in the intervention. We present a template for scoring sub-scales in Table 4.1.

Overall scores can be used by therapists to estimate the approximate time that the therapeutic intervention may take. We present recommendations for therapy duration based on LAG-FQ total scores in Table 4.2.

Treatment in Action

How do we select what kind of intervention for what kind of presenta-tion? How can we understand if the intervention suits the purpose and is fit for the purpose? This is based on understanding that the client could be traumatised as well as experiencing loss, the two conditions are dis-tinct from each other and they need to be dealt with individually. The need for assessment of presenting difficulty at this stage is crucial, for example a client reportedly indicating that they have intrusive thoughts about their loss, in contrast to intrusive thoughts about the event when they experienced loss. The latter relates to a specific event that was experienced as traumatic, whereas the former refers to intrusions about the loss itself and the meaning attached to the loss.

We draw a clear distinction between the loss (solving the problem of loss) and the trauma (event). The language of intrusion is perhaps limited here to distinguish between the two. The word "intrusion" is limited in this context. We think about "stuckness" here instead – are they stuck? Or are they having trauma intrusions? Stuckness refers to loss-related intrusive thoughts which are about solving the problem of the loss. Trauma intrusions are more similar to a post-traumatic stress disorder (PTSD)-presentation with flashbacks and reliving of the events surrounding the loss itself. It is likely that a person may present with both of these experiences – both trauma intrusions and loss-related stuckness.

Following assessment, formulation, and case conceptualisation, sometimes the client has an idea of what would work best for them – trust them in this. You're containing the information so that they can come to the conclusion themselves. It is crucial for the client to have a clear idea of the intervention and the processes which enables them to foresee their progression and the stage of work they are operating on. The main focus at the beginning of the intervention part of treatment is to understand how we as clinicians can encourage clients to engage with the treatment. They may be ambivalent or staying within their learned helplessness as a form of protection against more painful and less socially acceptable primary emotions (e.g. disgust). We believe that this process begins during assessment and formulation, where the therapist reframes the client's experiences: this distress is the result of the brain's inability to solve the problem of the loss. Taking this non-blaming and evolutionarily protective/positive approach is likely to normalise and validate clients' experiences in order to open them up to the possibility of exploring their loss and grief at a deeper level. Some people may be caught in the stuckness as they won't want to lose the person – but this begs the question "what now?". We suggest that through assessment, formulation, and case conceptualisation, both clinician and client come to a recognition that the person has already been lost – and that what comes next is finding the best compromise for the client at this point in time which will reduce their distress and improve their functioning.

Loss is a change in itself – so a person needs to change to cope with the loss. The process of treatment is solely based on the ongoing assessment and discoveries of new information, reformulation of presentation and case conceptualisation. It is noteworthy to mention here that the essence of treatment is based on self-assessment and awareness of current challenges, progress and ongoing compromises that would enable the individual to be in tune with their approach to manage the loss and deal more efficiently with the grief.

Whilst previous understandings of managing loss and bereavement take a more passive approach with time being a healer, we believe that there are specific processes that are needed for one to be able to recover or cope better with loss and its subsequent difficulties. Here we propose an active approach in addressing the loss and speeding the process of recovery with such experiences, especially when an individual is faced with multiple or sequential losses.

If we reflect on the theoretical position of this book, it was postulated that we as individual and society have a primal and innate disposition that makes us more attuned with strategies used to improve our survival rate and therefore our success in managing the threats to our system. Simply, this is an attempt of constant internal evaluation and emotional processes that could help us to remain content or be happy. The main theme here is the method that an individual uses to survive or navigate a less distressing experience. In true terms, this is based on rumination or reflection which helps us to learn, anticipation of future challenges such as worries and present management of our feelings. The main theme developed in us all includes problem-solving skills; this has been directly linked to our survival, learning, and coping. We tend to observe, learn, and apply skills that enable us to overcome challenges, survive, and ultimately thrive. In the eventuality that a problem cannot be solved or has no solution that the mind is able to formulate, the only logical solution is to go back to the beginning and review the problem again. This has been evident in our ruminative and worry-based presentation. Therefore, the evolutionary view of loss and bereavement would be encapsulated by the fact that an individual constantly attempts to find a resolution to unsolvable problem, hence initial state of shock and distress which may last for some weeks or even months/years, the reflection on the process and event in an attempt to find a resolution, hence the question of why? And more importantly, finding a way forward and therefore anticipation of future with the loss and how this could be managed?

Pre-intervention Psychoeducation

We have developed a metaphor that may support clinicians in explaining the experiences of loss and grief, and the active process of intervention. This "motorway metaphor" is intended to be used as part of the psychoeducation provided prior to beginning intervention, and is based on a four-lane motorway.

We can think of someone who has experienced a loss and is feeling stuck or frozen in time as being in the leftmost lane of the motorway. They are stuck in traffic and unable to move, whilst drivers in the other three lanes are moving at different speeds and passing them by. Moving from one lane to another is incredibly challenging as the others are driving too fast; this means that the driver misses chances to change lanes through apprehension and fear. Even when the lane to the right of the driver is clear, they don't feel ready to change lanes – they are worried about missing something, or not being able to drive at the faster speed in the second lane. Hence they remain in their lane, even as they feel confused and frustrated and powerless in their situation. This is akin to the experiences of someone stuck in a state of heightened feelings and caught in the bridging principle.

Sometimes, an individual may change lanes in a haphazard manner, moving into the second or third lanes and changing speed rapidly to match the pace of other cars around them. However, this becomes overwhelming very quickly as they don't feel ready to go at this faster speed – it adds to their fear and distress. Therefore, they move quickly back to the first lane – which may further add to their feelings of helplessness or hopelessness about being able to get out of the situation. This scenario describes someone who may abruptly make changes or decisions in the aftermath of loss – perhaps due to the paradox of self, and pressures to act as others are acting – but it is not a sustainable change and hence they revert back to their original ways of coping. An example of this may be someone who has been socially isolated since the loss, but pushes themselves to attend funeral arrangements as expected in their community. However, once the ceremonies are over, they go back to their state of learned helplessness and withdrawal, as maintaining that level of functionality is currently beyond their capacity to tolerate the pain. In order to change lanes intentionally and sustainably, the person needs to have an increased awareness of the entire motorway with all four lanes, and more clarity about both their destination and the journey itself. If the individual has a better understanding of which lane they are in and which lane they want to be in, they have more control over when to speed up and when to slow down; when to switch lanes and when to remain in their own lane. This is what the first phase of the intervention focuses on – increasing awareness of the person's current functioning and experiences, and highlighting where they would want to be in the future.

Once a person has increased their awareness of their current levels of functioning, they are more able to shift into the second lane. Once in the second lane, the focus of the intervention is to increase awareness of what has changed in their life – the impact of the loss on their feelings and day-to-day functioning. The second lane therefore maps onto the second phase of the intervention. Once awareness is developed about what has changed, the individual has more choice and control over their decisions and the way they live their life. Moving into considering choice and control, values and motives correspond with the third lane in the motorway, which is a combination of the third and fourth phases of intervention. The individual is encouraged to consider the dilemmas they are currently facing and the best ways to compromise in order to actively move towards a more fulfilling life.

Once the individual has increased their awareness of the loss and resulting changes, and improved their capacity to tolerate distress, they are more able to focus on the meaning-making of the loss itself. This allows them to think about what is important to them and make decisions in their best interests – rather than remaining stuck in traffic on the motorway (bridging principle and paradox of self) when they could watch the road carefully and change lanes (actively making compromises) in order to move towards their preferred destination (values). The process of actively making decisions and acting on them in line with one's values and motives corresponds with the final phase of intervention. This is the fourth lane of the motorway: the individual needs to choose a strategy in order to manage the loss. There is an explicit focus on re-engaging with one's social network in order to begin feeling re-connected to others and re-establish relationships. This aids the grieving process and further enables the individual to improve their socio-occupational and emotional functioning.

Five-Phase Principles for the Treatment of Loss and Grief

In this section we intend to provide a five-phase protocol which an active method of approaching loss and grief. It is essential to consider that grief is a logical outcome of loss experiences, hence this should be considered within the process of recovery and development of skills in coping or compromising with the loss.

These phases are intended to gradually and gently guide the client through the active processing of their loss, in order to reduce their distress (grief), consolidate their values, and facilitate them in moving towards a meaningful future in functional ways. To begin with, we seek for people to reach a point of safety, develop skills to regulate emotions, and stay in a position of calmness to observe their thoughts. Relaxation and calming exercises need to be tailored to the individual (not one size fits all).

The next step is to recognise what has changed for them in order to understand how to manage distress and what resources/supports need to be accessed. The therapist may need to help the client in accessing community support and other resources available to them.

Lastly, the aim of intervention is to develop hope about there being an end to the pain. This positivity helps the person develop the motivation to learn skills to cope and to work towards moving forward. Therapists are encouraged to incorporate religion and encourage clients to seek support from religious leaders and communities. Customs and rituals can be beneficial – and can augment the process of help-seeking. This part of the intervention focuses on developing a sense of steadiness, calmness, and fostering hope. Therapists are encouraged to focus on helping clients to develop supportive and nurturing relationships.

Some people may not want to access support – not wanting to show they are struggling – and there may be a conflict between shame and pride. The pride can be so strong it prevents the person from accessing support. For example stiff upper lip attitudes in the UK, "get on with it," "you're okay" – statements that appear to be supportive but are actually attacking. Such narratives often make people feel ashamed – their pride then prevents them from expressing their distress, which further heightens suffering. When people are not able to function or deal with the change, then the social network forces them to "streamline their attitude" – which further compounds their problem, because they don't feel able to be a part of that social network authentically. It is important for the therapist to not only be aware of these narratives, but to explicitly name them in the thera-peutic space and to unpack the meaning and impact of such social ideas on the individual. This is a process that begins in assessment and formula-tion, and continues throughout intervention. Therapists who may struggle to detach from these narratives themselves are encouraged to use super-vision to work through their own socially constructed understandings of loss and grief in order to improve the quality of intervention for clients.

Treatment: Five-Phase Protocol

Phase One

The first phase of treatment focuses on listening to the client's narratives: past, present, and future. The clinician begins to introduce psychoeducation relating to the protective and threat systems when experiencing loss. This phase of treatment is intended to socialise the client to the model, increase their awareness of the impact of the loss, and improve their emotion regulation and distress tolerance skills. This begins with educating the client to notice, recognise, and name feelings using the Daily Feelings Log (see Appendix B). Once clients are skilled up in noticing and naming their feelings, they can begin to make links between emotions, feelings, thoughts, and behaviours (using the classic CBT hot cross bun model). Following exploration of thoughts, feelings, behaviours, and emotions, we encourage clinicians to use the Daily Log of Productive and Unproductive Activities (see Appendix C). This is intended to highlight the activities currently occupying the client's day-to-day life, and to shift the focus onto evaluating the practical functionality, psychological function, and emotional impact of each activity. This is intended to contribute to defusion from one's internal states and to lay the groundwork for clients to begin recognising helpful and unhelpful patterns of relating and coping.

In this phase of treatment, we encourage clinicians to be alert to noticing what is not being shared or discussed, the notion of "silent dialogue". This is explored in further detail in Chapter 5.

Phase Two

In the second phase of treatment, the clinician introduces the idea of past, present, and future challenges having an impact on the client's current wellbeing. This includes: rumination (recall and reflection of what has happened); anxiety, fear, or low mood (experienced currently); and worry (anticipation of challenges in the future).

Recognition of the concept of problem-solving in addressing the problems faced. Identifying and accepting the inability in finding a resolution would lead to further suffering (i.e. grief and its symptoms). We recommend that clinicians use the Daily Log of Rumination and Worry (Appendix D) to support clients in tracking their thought content, as well as the impact of these cognitive processes on their daily functioning and mood. This is intended to begin the process of upskilling metacognitive awareness, and hence set the scene for more active intervention in phases three to five of treatment.

It is in this phase of intervention that the bridging principle comes to life. The client is likely to be looping over in terms of oscillations between ruminating and worrying, with very little time spent in the present. Clinicians can ask questions to help clients notice this process (metacognitive awareness) and to defuse from the pattern. Questions such as "Can you solve this problem right now?", and "Do you have time to think about it right now?" can function to distance the client from the content of the thoughts, and shift the focus onto the process instead. This is similar to postponement techniques commonly used with obsessions and worries in second-wave CBT approaches. The client may feel a sense of responsibility to stay within the loop – thoughts such as "you have to feel bad" and "you have to feel uncomfortable" may act to maintain the looping over process.

Psychoeducation about the bridging principle is needed at this phase of treatment, as part of socialisation to the model. We recommend that clinicians begin by explaining the existence and function of the threat/protective system – in line with classical compassion-focused therapy (CFT) approaches, with the addition of the protective/positive functions of the threat system. Following this, clinicians can explain that the brain cannot deal with not knowing – it needs to know, and so because the consequence of the loss is unknown, the brain continually tries to solve the problem by looking through past experiences and projecting the self into the unknown future. However, since the future is always an un-knowable thing, the brain gets stuck – and hence reverts back to looking through past memories – therefore creating a loop. When the person is not aware of this looping process, they end up pushing themselves even harder to find the answer – therefore spending less and less time being present in the here-and-now, and more and more time in the past or the future. If the person asks "How am I going to live my life without that person?" – the brain becomes constantly preoccupied with this question and the person invests a lot of time to plan and think and solve this potential problem (fear of unknown, anticipatory anxiety). We develop lots of strategies to deal with this not-knowing – the most common of which is avoidance. Whilst this may seem to reduce distress in the short term, it actually maintains distress in the long-term as it prevents the person from addressing the real problem at hand – what has changed since the loss? And how can I continue living my life?

Tackling the bridging principles requires a style of questioning which aims to highlight the client's awareness of the looping pattern, and to disrupt the loop by introducing a new perspective (reframing). For example, clinicians can ask questions such as "Ask yourself, do I really need to know this? How will knowing the answer help me? What's the benefit of knowing?". These questions serve the double function of interrupting the looping process and also reassuring the brain that the person doesn't need to explore and solve this problem at this time.

We recommend an active intervention to disrupt the bridging principle using imaginal rescripting. Clinicians are encouraged to guide clients to imagine a future where the person can cope with the loss. For example someone who is worried about dying and leaving people behind. Create an imaginal script where the people left behind can survive and can be happy and laugh again. This is similar to nightmare rescripting – rescript until the mind understands that this can be survived. There is a need for the person to come to a resolution – that the loss has occurred, the ways in which it has affected them, and the fact that they cannot change the loss itself and hence must focus instead on how to cope. Imaginal rescripting begins this process by not only defusing from the bridging principle, but also resolving the need to immediately solve the problem. This increases the person's window of tolerance for remaining in the here-and-now, hence setting the scene for the next phase of intervention – noticing what has changed and developing ways to strengthen coping and resilience.

Phase Three

The third phase of intervention focuses on increasing awareness of what has changed, and the impact on individual, group, or social functioning. This includes reviewing the coping skills and levels of functioning and identifying resources that could be helpful to improve the current challenges. We recommend that clinicians actively consider and explore culture and customs that could be enabling or hindering for the individual. This phase also begins the development of self-compassion, especially with regarding permission-giving to oneself and others to tolerate the grief and begin the process of accepting the loss.

The third phase of intervention is characterised by an exploration of the paradox of self. This is a see-saw between self and others, where the individual is likely to be comparing themselves to others in relation to the loss, grief, and functionality. Clients may place themselves either above or below others: when the self is perceived as lower than others, others are experiences as being better off than the self – others are better able to cope, others are better people (e.g. a better child, better parent, and better friend). This can feed into cycles of learned helplessness, or anxiety/fear, punishing the person for not "matching up" to others, and hence deepening their distress. On the other hand, if the client sees themselves as better off than others – others are seen as lower than the self, perhaps others are less able to cope, less good at managing the loss, less good as a person. This can contribute to a narrative of the self always needing to meet those "better" expectations – to continue to "cope" and present in a "functional" way without showing any distress or "weakness". Therefore, this can also contribute to feelings of learned helplessness, anxiety/fear, and contribute to a person's distress. This axis may continually tilt – with the person oscillating between seeing themselves as better vs worse than others, further compounding confusion about one's selfhood and ability to cope – and hence further entrenching the stuckness.

It is the role of the therapist to unpick the paradox of self to support the client in noticing this process and its impact. This begins by providing normalising psychoeducation about the fact that all of us are constantly on this see-saw – tilting between self > others and others > self, and rarely reaching a balanced point in the middle. Psychoeducation needs to include an evolutionary perspective – explaining that it's a constant comparison and it's happening all the time. The reason to compare ourselves is because we want a better quality of life and a happier state of being. However, the catch is that the paradox of self is not based on factual information; individuals make a disjointed judgement or an incongruent judgement based on sparse information – most of it internal cues – "I feel inferior therefore I must be inferior" rather than evidence from the external world.

We encourage therapists to empathically challenge this paradox with the client, using questions such as "What actually needs to happen for you to see yourself as equal to other people? Whether that's to do with functionality? Earning?" and so on.

Intervention for the paradox of self goes back to the basic essence of second-wave CBT: Does the evidence match with your experience? If the evidence is clear that they're not function as well as the other person then – what do they need to function better? This way of exploring the paradox of self opens an opportunity to discover new skills and new ideas to improve the quality of life. The key point of this exercise is that we do not stop at noticing and naming the paradox. In this model, we actively challenge the paradox to create a shift in meaning-making. If someone truly is coping less well than others, then we don't challenge that – what we do challenge is the idea that they are therefore incapable of coping well. By skilling the client up in coping strategies, we create tangible evidence to challenge the idea that they are coping less well than others. We provide experiential evidence to counter the paradox, rather than trying to change the paradox itself.

Underpinning these are the rules for living and a simplified version of the cognitive triad. If the client's rule for living is "I am less than other people", then by definition they must always remain stuck at the bottom of the see-saw. When someone sees someone else doing what they want and getting on with their life, it makes the person feel debilitated or helpless – stuck in their lane and watching the other people in the other lanes driving by. However, we encourage clinicians to challenge this narrative by creating opportunities and affordances for the person to prove themselves wrong – to show themselves and others that they can cope better. In this way, we can move them along the see-saw to a more balanced position (whilst acknowledging that there will always be a tilting of the see-saw in all of us).

The paradox of self also operates at a collective socio-cultural level. For example, if you're white, you're raised to always think that you're better than people who are racialised. When a white client meets a therapist of colour they automatically see themselves as above. So this operates at a cultural level as well as an individual level. We recommend the use of supervision in cases where factors of power such as race, gender identity, ability, religion, and sexuality affect the therapeutic relationship. This is also a factor in the supervisor–supervisee relationship and is explored further in Chapter 5.

Phase Four

In the penultimate phase, intervention focuses on exploring options and considering methods whereby an individual, group, or society can come to terms with the changes and difficulties experienced. This involves expanding tolerance for the existence of the loss and initiating the sense of acceptance of what has occurred, and its impact on the past, present, and future dreams.

This phase also includes a review of the client's values in a longitudinal fashion, which can be an extension of the values-based assessment (see Chapter 2) or as a stand-alone task using the My Lifetime Values worksheet (Appendix E). This exercise is intended to highlight the natural changes in values, beliefs, and priorities over a person's lifetime and to encourage the client in taking an active stance in considering the values they wish to embody in the present and the future.

In this phase of intervention, we encourage clinicians to use the diamond formulation (see Figure 4.1) to support clients in understanding the interplay between key factors maintaining their distress.

This formulation diagram has been developed by the authors to guide clinicians and clients in exploring the key areas of conflict in relation to loss. These dilemmas typically remain unresolved, hence presenting as distress which can be prolonged and does not abate with time. By bringing the client's attention and awareness to these key factors, it is possible to actively shift out of the state of stuckness/freeze and to move towards a

Diamond Formulation

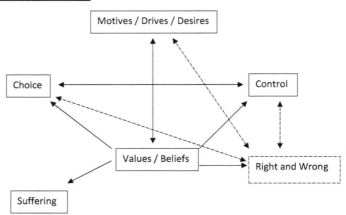

Figure 4.1 Diamond formulation diagram.

more meaningful and fulfilling life where the loss has been accepted and assimilated into the person's way of being.

The key parts of the diamond formulation are explained next.

MOTIVES/DRIVES/DESIRES

A person's motives, drives, and desires are factors that move them towards certain people, places, activities, and feeling states. This component is akin to the drive system as conceptualised by CFT. It is important to unpack what motives a person may have and where those motives come from – whether they are internal to their selfhood/identity/values or exter-nally influenced by the expectations or needs of others. There is no "right" or "wrong" set of motives; it is important to bring a compassionate and open stance to exploring a person's desires. In the context of loss, a person's desires may be in conflict with their sense of right and wrong, leading to painful feelings such as shame and guilt. It is sometimes easier to begin with the emotion and work towards drives/desires gradually – especially with individuals who present with significant emotion dysregulation and report a lot of shame. With individuals who have a greater preference for cognitive processing or who may be detached from their emotions, it is recommended that exploration begins with motives and drives, and moves gradually towards the associated feelings.

VALUES/BELIEFS

A person's values and beliefs are the core factors important to them. They inform a person's worldview and beliefs, and influence thoughts, feelings, and behaviours in the here-and-now. People's values are relatively consistent over time, but they may also change – especially in the aftermath of loss. It is important to examine values in the past, present, and projected values for the future as part of this formulation. The conflict between values and motives is likely to be resulting in significant distress in the context of loss. It is important to explore not just motives and values separately, but also their relationship with each other. For example, a person may value monogamy but after losing their partner they may desire physical or sexual intimacy. This desire may be experienced as directly contradicting the value of monogamy, and hence lead to a lot of shame and guilt. There is also an interplay with the person's sense of right and wrong, as they may make a moral judgement about the existence of their desires (e.g. I'm a bad person for wanting sex after my partner has died). Understanding the feeling here requires exploration of both values and desires, as well as the interplay between the two. Values also influence the degree of choice and control that a person feels they have and are able to exert in a given situation. For example, if a person values mindfulness, they may feel that they have to relinquish choice and control over their emotions – but in doing so, they remain frozen in time. To actively move towards alleviating their suffering would contradict the value of mindfulness and so can cause distress and/or confusion for the person.

CHOICE

Choice refers to a person's ability or capacity to make decisions about their life. In the context of loss, there are some elements which the individual has no choice over (e.g. how the person died) and other elements where they may be able to make choices in line with their motives and values. However, it is likely that the person is in a state of learned helplessness or freeze response, where they are not making choices about the things they *do* have choices for. For example, a person may feel that they have no choice in how the lost person is remembered, but they do have a choice about their role in this – whether that refers to how they relate to the person in their own mind, or how they influence funeral arrangements, and so on.

CONTROL

Control refers to the extent to which a person has the ability or power to influence a given situation. There are various factors that individuals have no control over, such as the time of death of a loved one. However, there are also many factors that people do have control over – such as how they relate to the lost person in their mind and how they lead their life in the aftermath of the loss. As noted earlier in relation to choice, control is also something that people may often feel they don't have at all – even in relation to factors which do remain in their control. For example, an individual may report feeling powerless and unable to do anything on the face of a loss. It can help, at this phase of intervention, to gently challenge this generalised form of learned helplessness to support the person in recognising their agency and control across different contexts.

RIGHT AND WRONG

This component in the formulation refers to a person's morality: their sense of right and wrong. Whereas in acceptance and commitment therapy (ACT) this is subsumed within values, here we separate right and wrong from values and beliefs. This is because a person's sense of what is right and wrong overlaps and intersects with their values. For example, a person may value compassion – and their moral sense tells them that this is the right way to lead one's life. So not only is compassion a value, it is also imbued with a sense of "rightness" or "correctness". A person's idea of what is right and wrong influences their desires and motives, and a conflict between morality and desire can lead to feelings such as shame. This moral compass influences how much a person feels they have choice and control in a given situation, as there may be internal judgements about how "right" or "wrong" it would be to exert more choice or more control in a given context.

Phase Five

The final phase of intervention is aimed at supporting the client to find an acceptable resolution – coming to a point of compromise or acceptance of the loss. This phase also consolidates the use of strategies in managing the change and developing ways of living in line with the new values for the future (developed in phase 4). It can be useful to consider the process of change, compromise, and acceptance using the finding a resolution diagram (Figure 4.2).

This diagram presents a visual representation of how the loss (conceptualised as change) leads to a process of problem-solving and compromise. Typically when individuals approach a therapist for support, it is because their way of finding compromise has led to a form of

Finding a Resolution

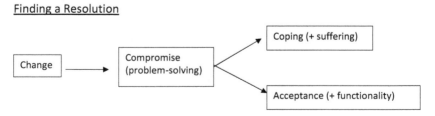

Figure 4.2 Finding a resolution diagram.

coping which is accompanied by and maintains their distress. The aim of therapy is to revisit the change (loss), compromises made (problem-solving approaches), and to guide the client towards the alternative outcome: acceptance which is accompanied by an increase in functionality. There is a subtle distinction here between coping and acceptance; when a person is coping, they are surviving but they are not truly living. When they move into a place of acceptance, they are genuinely living their life to the best of their capacity and in line with their values – a meaningful way of moving forward towards thriving.

Case Vignettes

In this section of the book, we will be providing some examples with themes that identifies the main core of the discussion and treatment in action, where therapist and client are able to have a clearly defined content to work through and therefore have an acceptable and compassionate outcome. Information about the case has been modified in order to keep the individual's identity confidential.

We hope that through these six case studies, we can demonstrate the ways in which the model can be applied flexibly based on the needs and functionality of the client. In some instances, people present with both trauma- and loss-related changes in functioning. For some individuals, the loss work needs to be done first and the trauma work second; with others, the trauma work needs to be done first before the loss work can begin. The clinician would need to decide on the order of intervention based on the person's presenting difficulties, the formulation and case conceptualisation, and the client's willingness and capacity to tolerate the work.

This model focuses on moving away from the symptom-based approach (which is what previous approaches such as the cycle of grief do) – towards discovery and finding a resolution to the reported concerns in relation to functionality. We are not being selective about symptom presentation – we want to find out how the person ended up here. When we formulate and develop a case conceptualisation, both the client and the therapist are discovering something together. We would like to highlight that the use of Socratic dialogue results in a process of guided discovery not only for the client but also for the therapist. This is the foundation of our model: the therapist taking a truly curious and not-knowing stance. The therapist is constantly discovering new information and gets surprised frequently, and continually adjusts our ideas and hypotheses. Whilst our model provides a framework for assessment, formulation, and intervention we do not intend that it is used in a rigid or prescriptive manner. Each client is different and each therapist–client relationship is unique; the process of the intervention is dependent entirely on the individual and relational factors in the therapeutic space and as such cannot be predicted or predetermined.

Case Study 1 – Harvey

Harvey is a 17-year old who identifies as a man and uses he/him pronouns. He was referred to therapy due to anger outbursts and intermittent periods of low mood, isolating himself, avoiding social interaction where possible, and frequent mood fluctuations. Harvey had previously completed bereavement counselling and trauma work. Harvey noted that the bereavement work involved the counsellor telling him about anger, bargaining, and denial – but his response was "I know. What am I supposed to do with that?". Furthermore, he did not believe that he was traumatised and felt that there was no change after the trauma work.

Phase I

During assessment it became evident that Harvey had a stable family and social network, and liked sports. But he has stopped being active since the news of his father's struggle with health. Later on in therapy, Harvey explained that his father was diagnosed with cancer and had not been given a good prognosis.

During initial screening, the LAG-FQ was reviewed with Harvey and from this information the therapist and client were able to identify a reduction in the degree of functionality, an inability to accept the current circumstances, and initiation of the process of grieving. Harvey's experiences were formulated as a two-stage loss: the first stage related to his level of functionality, relationships, and outlook on life – due to his father's sudden diagnosis. The second stage occurred after Harvey's father passed away when his levels of isolation increased.

T: tell me what happened.
H: I don't want to talk about it.
T: it must have been quite awful.
H: (emotionally charged, tearful). Yes it was. And it still is.
T: what would it be like if you could share that? (creating space to share a little background information)
H: I don't know.
T: okay. If you could at least tell me something about that experience, what would it be? (gathering information)
H: my dad died.
T: what happened that led to his death?

The aim of the intervention was to increase Harvey's awareness of what had changed, to help Harvey understand his emotional triggers, and for him to become more emotionally intelligent. The intervention also aimed to allow Harvey to understand at what point he oscillated between emotional triggers. In the first session following screening and assessment, Harvey spoke about how his life used to be and how it was now, as well as the transition between the two – especially in relation to the causes of his emotions. One of the first activities Harvey was asked to do was to label his feelings at any given time, using the Feelings Log.

The second task Harvey completed was an Activity Log to better understand the amount of time he was investing in different activities, and how those activities affected his mood. He reported doing things like watching TV, but feeling numb – not deriving any pleasure from such activities. In other words, Harvey was frozen in time with the loss event.

T: if you could say how you feel right now, what would that be?
H: numb. I feel numb.
T: okay. And do you feel like that a lot? Or is it just sometimes you feel like that? (exploring how much he uses detachment as a way to cope)
T: do you daydream a lot?
H: yes.
T: are you aware of it when you're daydreaming, or not? (making links between coping strategy and emotions)
T: what kinds of things have you done within the last 48 hours? (level of activity)
H: I was at home playing games or watching TV or YouTube.
T: do you enjoy doing these activities?
H: no. I feel numb.

Following psychoeducation and orientation to the threat system, and increasing Harvey's awareness of his inner states, Harvey was able to understand his difficulties and began to regulate his emotions more efficiently. Questions asked in these sessions included: What happened? What has gone on? Tell me about your life. Any more? How about your family members? Are you talking about this with anyone else?

Phase 2

After the degree of functionality and emotional markers had been identified, the therapist and Harvey needed to find out what cognitive components were activated. With Harvey, this was framed in terms of solving the problem: "if we were going to solve this problem, what are the key ingredients?" Harvey was oscillating between emotions and also between the past (rumination – father's diagnosis, prognosis, and the end of his life. This was associated with anger) and the future (imagining a future without his father – going to football games or playing in games without his father. This was associated with sadness).

There was a cognitive specificity for Harvey – thoughts of the past were associated with anger, and thoughts of the future were associated with sadness. The aim of this phase of treatment was to identify key emotional triggers and cognitive material that is looking for cognitive specificity; lots of different cognitions may generate the same emotional response.

T: when you feel like that, what kind of thoughts do you have?
H: this is unfair. I hate everyone who's lucky who still have their mum and
      dad and can do what they want to do. (paradox of self)
H: everyone else is better off than me.
T: how do you measure that?
H: I don't know. (common response when brain is overwhelmed with
      answering an unanswerable question – therapist needs to recognise
      that it's better not to go there)

After the client has become aware of the content of their thoughts (rumination and worry), the intervention focuses on increasing their ability to discriminate between the past and the future – and to increase their ability to tolerate and be present in the here–and-now. With Harvey, this was achieved by using techniques helping him to deal with rumination and worry, following classic second-wave CBT techniques. The end goal of this is for the person to recognise that there is no solution to the problem – that the ultimate aim of rumination is to learn and the aim of worry is to plan (to anticipate things that might go wrong and to fix those problems before they occur). The aim was for Harvey to come to the understanding that it's an impossible task to solve this problem – no matter how many hours he spent in reflecting or planning. This led to Harvey completing the two-bucket Rumination and Worry Diary. He identified how much of his time he spends in the past and the future. This task showed that the majority of Harvey's time was spent in rumination and an inability to accept the change.

T: so when you're sitting there and not doing anything, do you think about
      anything specific?
H: I think about my dad.
T: okay. What about your dad?
H: thoughts about what happened come into my mind when I don't want
      them. (typical of someone looping over – unable to find an answer to
      the problem – bridging principle)

Phase 3

Ultimately Harvey needed to come to the position of looking at the here-and-now, and the therapist needed to encourage Harvey to accept that what has happened has happened. In order to do this, Harvey needed to learn to compromise:

T: in order for us to move on, we need to figure out what has changed.
H: everything.
T: have you changed house?
H: no.
T: have you changed your friends?
H: no.
T: okay. Tell me exactly what has changed in your life.
H: I don't go play football. I don't socialise anymore. I don't play games with my dad. I don't go to watch football matches (extracting a list of activities he has stopped doing)
T: how many of these things are you able to do on your own? How many of them can you not do?
H: if I had my dad here, I could go to football (exploring reliance/dependence on the lost person)
T: if that's the case that you can do X,Y,Z, and we know you can't solve the problem of the loss of your dad – what would be the best compromise here?
H: I don't want to forget my dad.
T: by going and playing football, does that mean you forget your dad?
H: (laughs) that sounds so ridiculous.

Following this conversation, there was planning for a gradual acceptance. Harvey would increase his activities, but he wouldn't forget the time he spent with his dad doing those activities. So, his dad was in a way keeping him company during these activities.

This was the end of the intervention with Harvey (the therapeutic ending is not discussed here as the approach used was similar to second- or third-wave CBT). As noted in earlier chapters, not all clients begin at the same phase of treatment (due to their own processing of the loss prior to seeking therapy), and not all clients require all five phases. The phase of treatment to begin with, the order of phases, and the phase with which to end therapy are guided by the formulation and case conceptualisation and in collaboration with the client.

Case Study 2 – Julie

Julie is a 46-year old who identifies as a woman and uses she/her pronouns. Julie was born and raised in Southeast Asia and met her partner Becky whilst travelling. After their marriage, Julie and Becky resided in the UK. Julie had initially accessed therapy following a road traffic accident. As the trauma reprocessing work was nearing its end, Julie contacted the therapist about the sudden death of her wife. As Julie was already known to the therapist, the therapeutic process had a slightly different flavour in comparison to a new referral where the therapist and client do not know each other at all.

Phase I

In the first session, Julie explained what had happened in relation to her wife's death. Julie was at home; her wife Becky had gone out cycling on her own and had died on the roadside following an unexpected heart attack. A passer-by had phoned emergency services, and Julie only found out what had happened when police knocked on her door to inform her of Becky's death. There was a traumatic nature to this loss, as it was completely unexpected – Becky was in her early 50s – and there was the added shock for Julie of seeing police at her front door.

In the assessment phase, a thorough examination of current mental state was conducted. The therapist focused on identifying the degree of functionality and administered the LAG-FQ. The clinician also assessed how well Julie was coping, and what skills and resources she had. Julie reported difficulties with her finances, worries about her migration/residence status in the UK, and significant social isolation and loneliness. It is common practice to ensure that the client's basic needs are being met (Maslow & Lewis, 1987) prior to commencing with therapeutic intervention. Therefore, the first few sessions of Julie's therapy were spent in exploring her financial and housing difficulties, and supporting her in coping with the distress caused by these experiences.

T: what has changed in your life since the loss?
J: my home is at risk. My work is at risk. My finances are at risk.

Julie's main concerns related to: (1) being able to afford the mortgage on a single wage and the potential for being made homeless, and (2) being at risk of deportation by the home office due to lack of indefinite leave to remain in the UK. Both of these issues were directly related to the loss: Becky's presence had allowed Julie to live comfortably in the house they had jointly bought, and there was a financial security in their dual-income household which Julie was suddenly having to cope without. Second, Becky's presence ensured that Julie could remain in the UK without concerns about her migration status or paperwork. Julie was eligible for indefinite leave to remain, but had not felt the need to apply for this given that she was legally married to Becky. This became a challenge for Julie to navigate only after – and because of – Becky's death. Julie was experiencing a lot of fear and worry in relation to these difficulties with finances and residence status.

Following stabilisation of her financial and housing situation, Julie and her therapist began to focus more on the emotional and social impact of the loss, and the subsequent consequences for her levels of functioning.

Phase 2

Julie reported a lot of anger about what happened to Becky and how it happened. When Becky left to go cycling it had been a typical/mundane event and so when Becky left she said "I'll see you later" and Julie said "yeah okay" without looking up from whatever she had been doing at the time. After Becky died, Julie felt intense anger towards herself for the missed opportunity – for not appreciating the moment, for not telling Becky how much she loves her, for not giving Becky a kiss before she left. Julie also felt guilty that she was not with Becky when she died and worried about how much time Becky may have spent in pain on the roadside prior to the emergency services arriving.

In relation to these feelings, Julie was experiencing significant worries about the future. She reported that she wasn't sleeping well because she was spending a lot of time thinking about what she'll do in the future without her partner. Julie also reported intermittent sleep, with nightmares about having police at her door and being deported. Julie was also reliving the moment that the police came to inform her and was coping by distracting herself or trying to push the memories away. In order to move forward in the intervention, it was felt that brief imagery rescripting work would be useful in supporting Julie to manage the distress associated with these events and experiences. Therefore, the therapist encouraged Julie to stay with the emotions associated with having the police at her door and used imagery rescripting to help her brain understand that the event has already ended and that she is safe – she has not been deported. This stopped the night-time intrusions and nightmares and improved Julie's sleep – which was essential to continuing the loss-based therapeutic work.

Phase 3

Although Julie appeared to be "functional" in terms of continuing to work and carry out daily domestic chores, her scores on the LAG-FQ were low, suggesting that her social and emotional functioning were significantly affected by the loss. The initial focus of sessions was to identify and label current difficulties, and to consider the impact of each problem on Julie's current degree of functionality. It became apparent that for Julie, losing Becky was not only about losing a partner, but also losing a lifestyle, social network, and the activities that they were engaged in together.

Julie was in touch with her family and friends in her country of birth, but found these relationships very stressful because there was a lot of pressure, and they were critical of her ability to make a life of herself. Whilst Julie was in touch with friends and family, she did not feel emotionally connected to them or supported by them when Becky died: she intense social isolation, demotivation, and loneliness.

T: let's try to find out how alone are you. Tell me a little bit about your current life.

J: (described a lot of people being in contact with her, lots of people trying to reach out to her and communicate with her)

T: what is the role of these people in your life? What do they do?

J: my neighbours are a regular support. Every time I want help from them, they're available. But they're being careful not to interfere too much.

T: okay who else?

J: Becky's friends have been in touch.

Following this conversation, it became clear that many people were trying to stay in touch with Julie and to support her – but that she was feeling too overwhelmed by her worries to notice these points of contact. The therapist recommended that Julie complete a Daily Activity Log focusing specifically on social contact: Julie was invited to notice the total number of hours she was in touch with different people each day, what kind of contact she was having, and how it was impacting her mood. In doing this task, Julie became more aware of the extent of her social network – the number of people who were reaching out, and the way that these moments of connection helped her to feel slightly less alone and less overwhelmed.

Overt time, Julie began to report that her neighbours had become a good supportive network for her. They seemed to notice that she was losing weight rapidly – she wasn't looking after herself, wasn't eating or drinking. When Julie was younger, she had an eating difficulty (anorexic cognitive tendencies), so over her lifetime she managed periods of stress by restricting her eating. This was linked to the idea of self-worth and belonging and was linked to childhood experiences of being bullied for being gay.

The main focus of the intervention was to support Julie in improving her functioning across multiple areas of her life. This began with encouraging Julie to eat and drink in a regular way that would support her physical and mental health. Efforts to improve Julie's eating habits were complemented by her growing relationship with her neighbours. One of them had said to Julie that "I've noticed you've been losing weight since it happened. I know it's hard but you need to keep eating and drinking". This had a strong impact on Julie, as she realised that her long-standing difficulties with eating were still a part of her life and not a coping strategy that she wanted to continue using in the future. This strengthened Julie's motivation to change her diet habits through therapy.

Phase 4

The fourth phase of the intervention focused on Julie's relationship with Becky, and how she was feeling about the possibility of having another sexual or romantic partner in the future. Julie spoke about a big change in her life since the loss being the absence of physical contact and intimate connection which she shared with Becky. Not having this type of connection was adding to her loneliness. However, when Julie had asked friends about the possibility of connecting with someone else, her friends had strongly discouraged her – saying "it's too soon". This made Julie feel guilty for thinking about starting a new relationship or for wanting physical intimacy. There was also an internal block for Julie to begin the process of meeting someone new: she was remembering Becky as a "perfect" or "ideal" partner, and so even in her imagination, someone new would never match up to these expectations. Understandably, this was also deepening Julie's feeling of loneliness – that "no one will ever be the same" or that "I'll never be able to find someone who makes me happy like I was with Becky". The therapist used a gently challenging style to question this idealisation of Becky, shift some of the black-and-white thinking, and invite Julie to consider the possibility of having a romantic or sexual partnership in the future.

T: you know during your time when you met Becky and you got on, I assume you had lots of good times.

J: yes.

T: did you ever have any bad times? Tell me a little bit about those bad times.

Asking this type of question can be useful when working with the loss of a partner; the idealisation of the lost partner is a common coping strategy that many people use. It protects the memory of the person, seemingly justifying the depth of the pain experienced when that person is no longer with us. However, as stated above – this can also become unhelpful in the long term as it can prevent the person from engaging meaningfully with the relational and intimate aspects of their life. By asking questions that challenge the perfectness of the lost partner, we are able to invite clients to re-think and re-evaluate the relationship – we essentially contaminate the idealised image and reintroduce ambivalence as a way of supporting the process of acceptance and actively moving forward. There was also not much need to process guilt with Julie because that quickly washed away as soon as the therapist asked "is the relationship all perfect?". Comparing the perfect idea of someone to the reality of life leads to a contamination of the idealised version, and removes responsibility or blame on self – takes the burden away to also be the "perfect" partner in mourning who does not think about or want intimacy with someone new.

T: was your relationship with Becky all perfect?

J: no, of course not. We argued and fought just like everyone else.

T: is anybody perfect?

J: no. I'm not perfect and Becky wasn't perfect either.

T: what about other people?

J: no. nobody is perfect.

T: so what do other people have to be like for them to be a part of a new beginning for you?

J: well, I want to consider a new beginning because I feel really lonely. But other people are saying things like "when I lost someone, I didn't have a relationship for years." This makes me feel terrified about being alone for years.

T: okay. What would it be like to live by your own standards? To think about how you want to live, and live by your rules of living. But those rules have to be flexible enough that they won't harm you.

J: I can't imagine being with someone else physically – I feel disgusted with myself thinking about it.

T: okay. Is that your idea, or is that something you've heard from someone else?

J: my friend told me that's how they felt. It makes me feel like it's wrong to want physical intimacy with someone else. I feel disgusted with myself and guilty for wanting those things.

T: so when you met up with your partner Becky, the first time you met her, did you want to have a physical relationship with her?

J: no, the first time we met we just wanted to spend time together. Sex wasn't in my mind.

T: okay. So what expectations would you have for a potential partner?

Mechanical/physiological disgust (i.e. the nausea we feel when we see rotting food) has a significant and beneficial evolutionary response – it aids survival by preventing us from engaging with physically harmful things. Socio-psychological disgust, on the other hand, is socialised by dominant narratives within our cultures and is typically experienced when there are certain normative values or unspoken rules which an individual is expected to adhere to. The disgust that Julie described links to a socio-psychological response and not a physiological one; therefore, it can be challenged in therapy. Julie was already thinking about the latter part of a relationship (sex) before even meeting anyone.

The therapist was able to highlight this, and the compromises involved in the process of selecting partners using a grocery metaphor:

T: Imagine that you're going to the shop to get tomatoes for the first time in your life. How do you know which tomatoes you want?

J: I'll look at them, handle them, and buy the ones which I think look the best.

T: okay, so imagine that the next time you go to the shop, they don't have that exact type of tomato. Does that mean you're never going to buy tomatoes again?

J: well a relationship is not like tomatoes!

T: you're right, but the process of selection is almost identical. If you pick something up and you enjoy it, you go back to it. Next time, if you can't find what you had before, you look for something similar enough and you take a risk. It's a proportional risk – you can't be fully sure, but you can make an educated guess. Is the risk of picking a slightly bad tomato worse than the cost of never eating tomatoes again in your life?

Phase 5

The process of therapy needs to be fluid to meet the needs of the client. With Julie, the first part of treatment involved identifying key problems and addressing core physical safety needs. Following this, there was a process of identification and clarification of emotional and relational difficulties, which led to increased awareness of the changes that had occurred since the loss and the impact of these changes on current functioning. This was followed by psychoeducation about the bridging principle and supporting Julie to learn new techniques to reduce the amount of time she spent ruminating and worrying (not described in detail in this case study). There were elements of trauma-focused CBT embedded within the approach to support Julie's emotion regulation by using memory rescripting to reduce the distress and change the meaning of her encounter with the police. This was done as it was affecting Julie's sleep, which in turn was reducing her functionality both at work and at home.

The final part of intervention focused on unpacking the short- and long-term meanings of the loss, and exploring the potential for Julie to return to "normality". This included a longer conversation about what the barriers would be to Julie returning to a semblance of normality. Julie spoke about the conflict she felt in seeking support and advice from others who may then provide suggestions that added to her distress. It was important for the therapist to discuss the paradox of self with Julie at this stage and to provide psychoeducation about the impact of always placing herself below others – it led to her taking on others' advice even at a cost to herself, and so maintained or heightened her distress at a time when she was already feeling overwhelmed. The final phase of therapy also involved the therapist encouraging Julie to take more proportional risks, identify what she needs to do to be able to accept what has happened and begin to take active steps in moving forward.

Eventually Julie joined a dating app where she made various connections, met up with someone online, and then met them face to face. In the last session of therapy, Julie was considering spending more time with one of the people she had met in this way.

Case Study 3 – Seamus

Seamus is a 68-year old who identifies as a man and uses he/him pronouns. He was referred to therapy due to the loss of his wife to dementia. Seamus' wife was assessed by a community team for dementia and admitted to a nursing home during the COVID-19 pandemic. This meant that Seamus was unable to have contact with his wife during the last months of her life; she later died whilst living in the nursing home. Seamus reported a lot of annoyance, resentment, and blame towards the system due to these experiences.

Phase I

In the initial screening, Seamus said "I wouldn't have minded dying at the same time as her." In this session, there was a narrative developed of Seamus' life with his wife and an exploration of his current functionality. Seamus reported feeling very lonely, that he had no support network, and felt that whenever he goes anywhere it feels odd/unusual because his wife is not there.

Although Seamus' wife wasn't well for a long time prior to her admission to the nursing home, having her next to him made Seamus more functional. He was fit and healthy for his age, with no other medical difficulties. Seamus had hobbies of playing golf and cycling, but had stopped doing these since his wife went to the nursing home. He spent most of his time in the house and only went out for grocery shopping. Seamus was encouraged by family members to go out and do more activities, but he didn't have the motivation to do so.

Seamus was very in tune with his primary and secondary feelings, but the main concern was that he didn't feel complete and felt very alone. During assessment the LAG-FQ was administered, and his scores were quite low – suggesting low levels of functionality. Overall, Seamus was struggling to come to terms with the idea of restarting his life without his wife. There is also a trend whereby people tend to glorify or idealise their partners after death, which can perpetuate the intensity of their loneliness and increase hopelessness.

T: you're describing a life that was almost perfect.
S: yes.
T: what was perfect about it? And what were the difficult times?
S: (after giving examples of positives) but yes we did argue at times. So it wasn't as perfect as I was imagining it to be.

These types of conversations allowed Seamus to create space in his inner dialogue about his wife, to acknowledge both the positives and the negatives of his relationship with her. In doing so, he was able to begin talking more openly about his experience of losing her, the feelings the loss brought up, and the impact on his day-to-day life.

Phase 2

т: what has changed?

s: I don't have anyone to talk to. I don't feel motivated to do anything.

The second phase of intervention focused on understanding the cognitive processes Seamus was experiencing, and supporting him to recognise and acknowledge the cognitive loop (bridging principle) he had been stuck

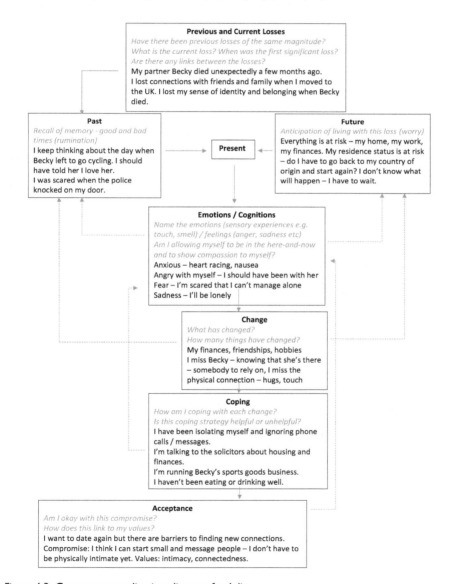

Figure 4.3 Case conceptualisation diagram for Julie.

in since the loss of his wife. Through the use of the Rumination and Worry log, it was identified that Seamus was stuck in rumination most of the time and that worry about the future played a smaller role for him.

When exploring the rumination a computer analogy was used to aid psychoeducation. Seamus came to understand that his brain was trying to reflect on what had happened in the past and looping to plan a positive outcome/find a solution – but as this was impossible, his mind was "rebooting" that is avoiding people, sleeping, staying in. This then led to a restart of the rumination – so he was stuck in the past and unable to find a way out. This recurring rebooting process was mentally exhausting and leaving very little energy for Seamus to engage with his support network (family) or activities that he used to enjoy and which supported his physical and mental health.

Phase 3

One of the main reasons that Seamus was caught in this stuckness was his belief that to reach out for support would mean burdening his family. He had always held onto the idea of himself as "strong", "capable", and "independent" – therefore asking for help contradicted his ideas of himself and contributed to his feelings of helplessness. Through conversation with the therapist, Seamus came to the realisation that in order to cope with the loss of his wife, the only strategy he had was to withdraw – not talk about it. He also spoke about the main source of his distress being related to the loss of physical touch, such as holding hands and hugging. One of the tasks in therapy was to think about touch/contact with his wife and compare this to touch/contact with other people in his family. Through this, Seamus was able to gradually reconnect with his family and to receive touch/physical contact from them.

Phase 4

One of the main reasons that Seamus struggled to process the emotional impact of the loss of his wife was the significant amount of anger he still felt towards the system for taking her away from him and preventing him from seeing her during the last months of her life. The penultimate phase of therapy focused on validating Seamus' anger and the blame he felt towards services. Following this, the therapist gently began to challenge the usefulness of this anger for Seamus in the here-and-now and in the future.

- Validation of anger and validation of blame – and then what's the consequence of that? What's the compromising position with those emotions? Discovering what's the best type of response with what he feels and thinks. Seamus' compromise was that if he can go and visit his wife multiple times a week, then he has given his respects, and talked to his wife to soothe his anger and pain. Over time, this reduced – he went once per week.

s: I feel so angry and guilty. I should have done more (biased sense of responsibility)
T: what could you have done?
s: nothing.
T: what's the consequence of holding onto this anger and blame for you?
s: I just can't forgive them.
T: what's the best compromise? what are the options now?
s: I'm going to go to the graveyard everyday to visit her.
T: does going there help?
s: yes.

The therapist encouraged Seamus to consider the best course of action in this situation, where his anger and resentment were justified but did not lead to any useful change in his life. He noted that the best compromise would be to visit his wife as often as possible to feel close to her and to help him feel better about not being with her in the last months of her life. Going to visit his wife regularly helped Seamus to express and process his anger and pain. Over time, he visited less frequently.

T: what has changed? Do you talk about the same topics? What is the outcome? Have you found your peace?
s: actually nothing is changing. And nothing is going to change. But I've said what I wanted to say.
T: so, do you have to visit the graveyard every week?
s: not anymore.
T: do you think your wife would be able to hear you anywhere you are, or does it have to be at the graveyard?
s: I can talk to my wife any time I want, I don't have to go to her grave.

This process of coming to the understanding that we can speak to someone we've lost, as a ghost or image, is itself a form of compromise. The brain finds a solution by creating access to their presence even in their absence – this is the brain not being able to cope with not-knowing, and hence it creates an answer to make it all make sense. It's an adaptive resolution to accept the distress that was caused. The brain does this naturally – as therapists, we may do it more purposefully when we engage in techniques such as imagery rescripting.

Phase 5

The final phase of intervention focused on supporting Seamus to re-engage with his family, daily activities, and life more broadly. Seamus had been in the War as a young man, so the therapist used the metaphor of being at war to encourage Seamus to reengage with his life.

T: everything is like a war. You have to win a small ground and move forward – looking for the "little wins".
S: I want to start tidying up the house. I have so much stuff I want to get rid of.
T: that sounds like a good way to start making some "little wins".

Seamus spent a fair amount of time going through each room in his house to keep the things he wanted and give the rest to charity. The last part of this process was to look through his wife's belongings, which was understandably the most difficult part. Gradually, Seamus was able to look at his wife's remaining clothing and belongings, to sort through them. By then, he was also much more engaged with his family and he asked his daughter to help.

Case Study 4 – Rachel

Rachel is a 28-year old who identifies as a woman and uses she/her pronouns. Rachel was referred to therapy due to work-related stress. In the initial sessions, Rachel did not want to discuss anything other than work-related issues, and the therapist experienced her as being guarded against other topics of discussion. Due to this, the therapeutic work began by increasing Rachel's window of tolerance for distress, and increasing her skills in emotion regulation.

Phase I

It was in the process of introducing and practicing emotion regulation skills that Rachel began to open up about past experiences which were affecting her in the here-and-now. She reported that her mind kept returning to past negative experiences during mindfulness activities and that this was paradoxically increasing her distress rather than reducing it.

T: there's a possibility that this is related to the past, and previous experience – which influence your ability to regulate your current emotions.
R: since I started doing the mindfulness, I've been more distracted by my thoughts.
T: what are those thoughts?
R: I don't know. I can't explain it.
T: can you provide a bit of a background to what these thoughts are related to? How long ago?
R: I had a miscarriage about a year ago.

   When the LAG-FQ was administered, it became clear that Rachel was highly functional – going to work, looking after the household, and so on. But because she was staying on task and keeping herself highly busy, she was not processing her past painful experiences. When this was brought to Rachel's attention, she was ambivalent about talking about her past experiences. This initially appeared to be avoidant in presentation, but the reality was that she had found that keeping busy was the best way to cope with and manage these distressing events. There was an unwillingness to explore the miscarriages in detail because she felt it was too painful. Through further questioning, Rachel explained that she hasn't talked about what she's thinking or feeling about the miscarriages with anyone – not even her partner, as she couldn't bring it up with him and he didn't ask her either. Rachel mentioned that they had briefly talked about it at the time of the event, but they hadn't explored it – it was felt to be too painful to discuss. Even if Rachel wanted to discuss her experience of the miscarriages, he was not willing to go there – he was more avoidant than she was.

T: tell me about your first miscarriage. What was it like at the time? What happened? Who was around? (gathering information)
R: (angry)
T: I can see that you're angry with me. What're you angry with me about?
R: you're annoying me because you're talking about things I don't want to talk about.
T: okay. What do you want to do? Do you want to keep this problem to yourself, or do you want to work through it and hopefully we can find a resolution?
R: I'm scared I won't be able to cope. I'm going to have a nervous break-down. You'll make me unwell.
T: there is nothing there that you don't already know.
R: (pause) that's true. There's nothing there that I don't know.

   It gradually came to light that Rachel had had four miscarriages in total. The most recent one seemed to be a traumatic event, as Rachel had had a stillbirth and required an operation to remove the baby from her womb. This was accompanied with a lot of blood loss, and there were medical complications that could have prevented her from having a pregnancy in the future. Therefore the intervention shifted to focusing on preparing Rachel to be able to face the loss – scaffolding her to be able to tolerate the emotions and see what has happened. Someone who is highly functional might appear to be okay, but underneath that narrative there may be different layers of loss of function. As a therapist, we sometimes meet with people who come with a seemingly "simple" difficulty, but once we engage with them you discover so many layers underneath which require careful and compassionate exploration.

Typically, the second phase of intervention focuses on exploring cognitive processes to increase the client's metacognitive awareness of rumination and worry as maintaining their current distress. For Rachel, there were three main reasons for not wanting to talk about her miscarriages: (1) fear of what it was like; (2) worry about how she could tolerate the distress of talking about it; and (3) shame and embarrassment about what had happened.

Rachel was unwilling to talk about her miscarriages at all – let alone participate in trauma reprocessing which would enable her to move forward from these experiences and towards a meaningful life. Therefore, intervention needed to address these three issues first to prepare Rachel for trauma reprocessing. The first two concerns fall within Phases 2 and 3 of the Five-Phase Principles model. The third concern is linked to values and culture, which relates to Phase 4.

Phases 2 and 3

Fear arises when something happens which threatens the integrity or safety of the self, and the individual is required to deal with that threat. Even after the threat has "ended" (e.g. the incident of a miscarriage has ended), it can leave remnants of fear in the person's mind – "this happened to me" – which continue to cause distress. In working with Rachel, this fear was taking over her ability to make choices about her wellbeing – she was stuck because of the fear of events in the past. The Five-Phase Principles model is based on the development of a strong therapeutic relationship where clinicians take relational risks (Mason, 2005) in asking difficult or confronting questions in order to support clients in actively moving from a place of stuckness to a place of functionality.

When Rachel said that she's scared to talk about her experiences because she couldn't face the fact that "this happened to me", the therapist encouraged the client to reframe their statement into: "yes it did happen, and I survived, and I'm here and safe now". We acknowledge that some clients may respond to this by saying "yes, but…" and provide other reasons for continuing to carry the fear. With Rachel, introducing the idea that she already knows everything that has happened to her was sufficient to shift her fear about talking about it. With others, exposure to the fear of talking about past experiences may require "talking about talking" (Macaskie et al., 2015) – speaking about what it would be like to talk about the experience, what skills they may be able to use to cope, what the therapist can do to support the conversation, what might happen after they have spoken about their experiences and so on. This helps to ease the person into the idea that they can talk about the "problem" without it overwhelming them, therefore warming the context (Burnham, 2018) for more specific second-wave CBT-based interventions around facing the fear and developing coping skills.

This leads to Rachel's second difficulty: the worry that she cannot cope with talking about her experiences. Once the client is ready to talk about their past, they may still feel apprehensive about their ability to cope with this. In such cases, the best way to address the fear is to support the client in facing it in a safe and graded manner and to develop skills in managing the fear when it arises. This is in line with typical second-wave CBT techniques for working with fears and phobias.

For Rachel, there were many worries in anticipation of the conversation about her past miscarriages, and she held firmly onto the idea that to talk about her experiences would make her have a "nervous breakdown" and ultimately make her "unwell". This was largely reinforced by her coping style, which focused on distracting her from her pain by keeping herself busy with work and other engagements in order not to allow difficult feelings to enter her consciousness. In line with the relational risk-taking mentioned earlier, we recommend that in such instances the therapist can gently remind clients that they have already been coping with their pain for a long time without help – they are already tolerating the distress, and there is nothing in the content of the memories which they don't already know or haven't already survived. The only difference between keeping it to themselves and talking about it in therapy is the creation of an opportunity for them to figure out which parts of those experiences are keeping them stuck, and how they might be able to get themselves unstuck from the pain.

Phase 4

The third of Rachel's concerns was the shame and embarrassment she was experiencing in relation to her miscarriages. The discomfort of these feelings was preventing her from engaging with those experiences and hence acting as a barrier to trauma reprocessing work in therapy. These feelings were also maintaining Rachel's stuckness in relation to her losses, as she could not process the meaning of the loss itself separately from the social evaluations leading to shame and embarrassment. These are two feelings which may arise due to a person's internalised values, and/or due to values related to their culture, society, religion, or spiritual beliefs. Therefore, when clients present with shame or embarrassment, we need to shift to values-based working.

The core of the difficulty here is the conflict between morality, desire, and right and wrong – presented in the form of criticism. At its core, this is about the critical thoughts the person has, and where they come from. For Rachel, much of her sense of shame and embarrassment was being fuelled by her religious community. This was occurring not due to other people's maliciousness, but due to Rachel's understanding of her own religion and her interpretations of others' comments. For example, if someone in her religious community said "that person doesn't know how to look after their child. They don't deserve to have a child" – she would make these into self-referential statements such as "maybe I won't be a good parent, and that's why God isn't giving me a child". This was related to core beliefs such as "I'm not good enough" and "I'm not deserving".

The therapist gently questioned these ideas with Rachel, asking questions such as "does the criticism help you? If so, in what way?". This was intended to ask for advantages of critical thoughts (e.g. as motivation for performing and maintaining one's internal standards), and to understand how generalised the critical thoughts had become over time. For Rachel, these thoughts had begun as useful motivators in relation to work and had quickly been taken up in other aspects of her life and identity – becoming an unhelpful default response in any situation with an unachievable challenge, therefore creating significant shame, embarrassment, and guilt in various parts of her life.

Trauma Work

Following this exploration of where Rachel's feelings of shame and embarrassment originated from, she felt more able to proceed with a Narrative exposure therapy (NET)-based retelling of her miscarriages. During the narrative work where she described each miscarriage in turn, Rachel's highly critical inner voice became prominent. It was clear that each event was interpreted in a self-referential way, such that she felt that she was to blame for each miscarriage.

R: it must have been my fault. It must have been me.
T: what gives you the sense that it was your fault?
R: f I haven't been able to have a baby that God gave me, then it must be my fault for losing the baby.

As this theme of religion in relation to blame and shame arose repeatedly, Rachel explored her relationship to her religion and how it was impacting her in the here-and-now. Eventually, Rachel decided that the best compromise to reduce the shame/embarrassment was to distance herself from the socio-cultural and religious community that was causing those emotions. Although this was not an easy course of action for her to take, it was a way for Rachel to re-establish safety for herself and move towards her values in a meaningful manner.

Following this conversation, the therapist drew on themes across all four miscarriages to explore the core meaning of the losses, using

Socratic dialogue to explore the meaning attached to these themes and experiences. For Rachel, it boiled down to "I'm not good enough." The therapist drew on imagery rescripting techniques (Arntz, 2012; Arntz et al., 2007; Arntz & Weertman, 1999; Brockman & Calvert, 2017; Holmes et al., 2007) to support Rachel in processing and updating early childhood memories which formed the basis for this schema. Rescripting memories of the miscarriages was a bigger challenge to explore than anticipated; Rachel did not feel ready to approach these memories directly for a long time. It was after more than 20 sessions of therapy that Rachel began to consider how she was feeling stuck in relation to the miscarriages and to begin considering what she wanted for herself in the future in relation to childbirth.

Phase 5

After 20+ sessions, she spoke about other medical interventions to be able to have a baby.

The last phase of intervention involved Rachel starting the conversation with her husband – about the potential of trying for another baby. That was the new beginning – her values had changed, and she could consider no other possibility. She seemed to be much more at ease after the conversation about loss, fear, avoidance, and early childhood experiences. Rachel seemed much more attuned to what she wanted, what she could do, and saw herself as much more able. She felt that she had more choice and control, that she hadn't felt before.

Case Study 5 – Faizal

Faizal is a 32-year old who identifies as a man and uses he/him pronouns. Faizal sought therapy due to experiencing the death of his father, mother, and brother within the space of three months. He was experiencing the aftermath of these multiple losses and struggling to cope with the distress and change in his functionality. Faizal's father died before the pandemic due to causes unrelated to COVID; however, both his mother and brother died due to COVID within a few weeks of each other. Faizal's mother was in a nursing home at the time of death, and Faizal was engaged in a dispute with the nursing home at the time of accessing therapy.

During the assessment, Faizal was encouraged to speak about each of the family members he had lost – what they were like, their interests and identities, and both positive and negative recollections about them. The therapist invited Faizal to speak about his relationship with each family member, with a focus on their desires and expectations for him. This formed the foundation for the conversation later in therapy about the impact of each person's loss on Faizal.

Phase 1

Through the assessment, it became apparent that Faizal felt a sense of guilt for spending more time thinking about the loss of his brother and his mother than his father; he felt that he was disrespecting his father by not thinking about him as much. This was the main feeling that he was

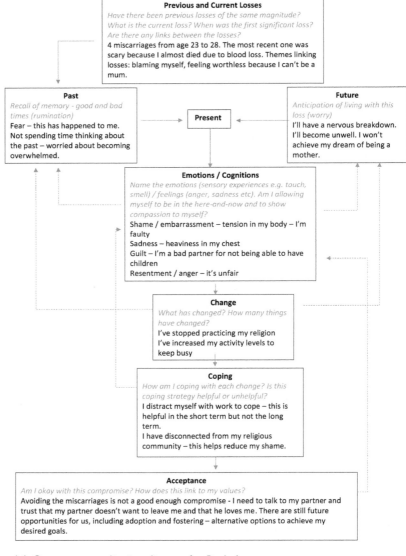

Previous and Current Losses
Have there been previous losses of the same magnitude? What is the current loss? When was the first significant loss? Are there any links between the losses?
4 miscarriages from age 23 to 28. The most recent one was scary because I almost died due to blood loss. Themes linking losses: blaming myself, feeling worthless because I can't be a mum.

Past
Recall of memory - good and bad times (rumination)
Fear – this has happened to me. Not spending time thinking about the past – worried about becoming overwhelmed.

Present

Future
Anticipation of living with this loss (worry)
I'll have a nervous breakdown. I'll become unwell. I won't achieve my dream of being a mother.

Emotions / Cognitions
Name the emotions (sensory experiences e.g. touch, smell) / feelings (anger, sadness etc). Am I allowing myself to be in the here-and-now and to show compassion to myself?
Shame / embarrassment – tension in my body – I'm faulty
Sadness – heaviness in my chest
Guilt – I'm a bad partner for not being able to have children
Resentment / anger – it's unfair

Change
What has changed? How many things have changed?
I've stopped practicing my religion
I've increased my activity levels to keep busy

Coping
How am I coping with each change? Is this coping strategy helpful or unhelpful?
I distract myself with work to cope – this is helpful in the short term but not the long term.
I have disconnected from my religious community – this helps reduce my shame.

Acceptance
Am I okay with this compromise? How does this link to my values?
Avoiding the miscarriages is not a good enough compromise - I need to talk to my partner and trust that my partner doesn't want to leave me and that he loves me. There are still future opportunities for us, including adoption and fostering – alternative options to achieve my desired goals.

Figure 4.4 Case conceptualisation diagram for Rachel.

reporting in therapy, as something causing him significant distress and affecting his ability to function well.

> T: why don't you try to ringfence and think about any one of them in a given day? So that you don't lose respect for any of them?

The therapist was attempting to support Faizal in improving his distress tolerance and emotion regulation skills. By asking Faizal to designate certain days for certain family members, the therapist was encouraging Faizal to postpone intrusions and worries – a skill which had the dual effect of increasing Faizal's window of tolerance and also allowed him to act in line with his beliefs about respect. At first, Faizal struggled to create these boundaries, but gradually as he practiced the skills of postponement, he found it really useful. Being able to respect each family member equally also led to a reduction in Faizal's feelings of guilt as well as decreasing the conflict with his values.

As part of this initial process of increasing Faizal's awareness and understanding of his feelings and values, a version of the ACT post-it note exercise was used. The therapist encouraged Faizal to think about the pain and distress caused by each loss separately and to link that pain with his core values and beliefs about the world. This helped to contextualise Faizal's pain and to further create distinctions between the impact of each family member's loss on his identity and functioning.

Phase 2

As Faizal began to work on managing how much time he spent thinking about each family member, it became apparent that he was thinking a lot about the responsibilities he had in the past, in the present, and what he would have in the future. A lot of these responsibilities related to these family members and what they would have wanted from him. The therapist encouraged Faizal to consider his responsibilities to each family member in turn and to make lists of his responsibilities for each of them.

> F: I feel really responsible for my brother's family.
> T: what type of thing do you feel you have responsibility for? Can you create a list of the things you feel responsible for in relation to your brother?
> F: to make sure his family is okay. To make sure his legacy continues.
> T: what else? What is your specific responsibility towards your brother himself?
> F: (thinking for a long time) well I'm not quite sure.

T: well, sometimes people choose to celebrate the person. Sometimes people choose to reflect and mourn. Sometimes people choose to have a moment of grief – or whatever that might be. What type of things would fulfil that responsibility for you? What would help you confirm that you've done your bit?

F: well if I was taking the western approach, I'd drink some whiskey to his memory – I think he'd like that,

T: that sounds like you're celebrating him, more than grieving

F: yeah I think so

T: okay, can you think about it some more and tell me next time about what else you need to do to reassure yourself that you've done the best that you can.

F: there's nothing else.

T: okay, shall we park that one and move onto the next person for now?

F: let's talk about mum.

T: what are the responsibilities?

F: she would have wanted me to pray. if I pray then she'd be happy with me.

T: how did you decide that's the best thing that your mum wanted for you? What gave you the idea that she wants it for you? She wanted it for herself, but how does that fit with what you want for yourself?

F: I have no idea.

T: okay, so is that the best compromise?

F: yes.

T: what about your dad?

F: he was a strong man who was responsible and looked after the family. He would want me to do the same – to be a reliable person who the family can depend on.

T: okay. Can you write down a list of all the things your family members would have wanted you to do? A list of responsibilities.

Phase 3

As Faizal spoke about the responsibilities he felt towards each family member, he also started to talk about what had changed in his life since he lost his father, mother, and brother. It was important to speak about each family member separately, as each had played a different role in his life, and hence their loss had different impacts on Faizal's wellbeing and functioning.

When Faizal's father died, as the eldest son he had to take on the responsibilities of the family business. Although this was a stressful transition for him, Faizal was always supported by his younger brother and so felt able to cope with this change. After Faizal's brother died, this became much more impactful for his functioning; he did not feel able to manage the business effectively on his own and did not know whom he could reach out to for support. In addition to this, Faizal felt immense responsibility towards his brother's wife and children, and felt that he needed to care for them in the absence of his brother. Due to this sense of responsibility, he felt more pressure in relation to the business and his own finances, as he also needed to care for his own wife and children as well. One of the "blessings in disguise" was that having so much to manage with the business helped Faizal to remain distracted from the pain of his multiple losses; therefore he appeared to be much more functional than he was for example he was still attending work and managing the business etc. However, when the therapist dug deeper, it became clear that Faizal was struggling to function – as reflected in his low LAG-FQ scores. He was experiencing significant intrusions about his father, mother, and brother during moments of rest, which was affecting his ability to sleep, and in turn increasing his agitation, distress, and paranoia about the business and finances.

Phase 4

Faizal was very occupied by his ideas of what his deceased family members would have wanted him to do, and the responsibilities he felt towards them. Therefore, the therapist used the diamond formulation diagram to create a diamond for each of Faizal's family members – father, mother, and brother. These were based on Faizal's ideas about each family member's motives, values, morality, choice, and control. These diagrams were then used to help Faizal to separate himself and his needs from those of his family members. The therapist encouraged Faizal to begin developing his own diamond formulation based on his identity and what was important to him; Faizal actively and intentionally began to integrate elements from each family member's diamond into his own, whilst retaining his sense of self and his agency in the process.

T: okay. For example, your dad wants you to work very hard, and your mum wants you to practice religiosity, and your brother wants you to drink whiskey.
F: (laughs)
T: so how can you meet all of these demands? what is the best compromise here to meet all of their expectations?
F: I'm not sure.... They seem to be very different from each other.
T: yes...How can you fulfil that responsibility for all of them? If you're going to practice religion, then how're you going to drink whiskey? Won't that contradict the other? And if you wanted to follow your brother's wishes of living life to the fullest and enjoying yourself, then you wouldn't be able to meet you father's expectations of being very dependable and reliable and always being there for the family.
T: so each of your family members had their own motives, values, choice, and control.
F: yes.

T: what about you? How much choice and control do you have over your values and motives?

F: not much, because I feel like I have to do what they would want from me.

T: how has this changed since your losses? These are other people's expectations for you. So what are your expectations of yourself?

F: I can't think of it like that. If I do, then I'm selfish and egocentric.

T: so on the one hand, you have people that have been lost. And on the other hand, you have people depending on you. So how much of your time/effort /energy are you willing to invest in both of these groups?

The therapist wanted to highlight that Faizal was currently using his energy ruminating about the past, rather than actively and positively using it for the benefit of the present and the future. The aim of ringfencing and compartmentalising his rumination about each family member was to help him postpone those ruminations as much as possible, in order to focus on the here-and-now and how he can manage his own dilemmas. To do this, he needed to consider and show his respect for each family member in turn, before being able to consider that he also has needs, desires, values, and motives which are valid and require addressing.

Faizal found the best compromise for himself: he took a piece of each person's motives and values, and put it towards living with his family and with his brother's family. This was his description of the best adaptive resolution – the idea was not that he shouldn't feel sad or upset, but that he had a greater task at hand to manage.

Phase 5

In the final phase of intervention, the therapist asked about the projected future:

T: when you don't have those responsibilities in the future (for example, when your children and your brother's children have grown up and are independent), how will you manage these challenges?

F: (laughing) I can divide the days of the week – 2 days to be like my dad, 2 days to be like my mum, 2 days to be like my brother, and 1 day to be like me.

T: it seems like you're quite uncomfortable about this – you're being quite jovial, but it's a serious topic we're discussing.

F: I don't want to feel bad.

T: okay, so why do you have to feel bad? How did you come to the conclusion that you should feel bad or should feel good?

F: my responsibility is for the people who are living right now. and when that changes – when the kids grow up and they don't need me in the same way – I can divide my time to other people so that I can meet their needs and fulfil my responsibilities.

Diamond Formulation

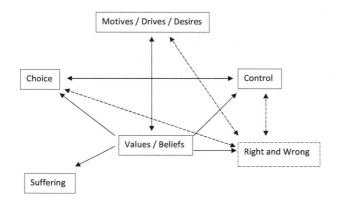

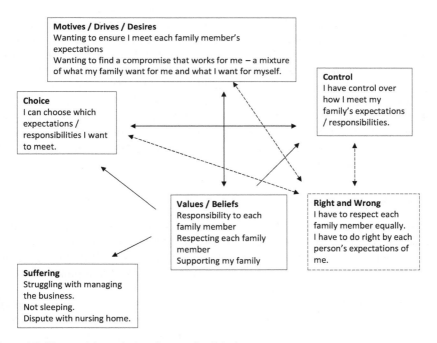

Figure 4.5 Diamond formulation diagram for Faizal.

This was how Faizal was trying to come to the conclusion that there's no right or wrong, and that he's doing the best that he can. One of Faizal's main dilemmas related to religion. His mother had been raised in a religious household, engaged with religious activities regularly and was active in the local Muslim community. However, Faizal's father had been raised in a less orthodox environment, and all three of the men in the family did not practice religion formally. This was causing Faizal a lot of distress since the death of his mum because he felt a responsibility to re-engage with Islam as a way to live up to her expectations of him. However, this was in conflict with his own values and worldview, and so he was caught in the looping over process of the bridging principle. Due to this, the therapist encouraged Faizal to seek the support of an Imam. Faizal spoke to an Imam about living and dying, and the loss of his mother. The Imam said "when your time is up, God wants you to join him", but Faizal found this really unhelpful – he felt that God might want it but I wasn't ready. Faizal felt annoyed and didn't find it soothing to hear that.

Eventually, Faizal came to the conclusion that he can fulfil his responsibility to his mum by living in line with her values around caring for others and being supportive, without having to become religious or develop faith in God. His compromise was to show his responsibility to her through his actions for example do a prayer in my mind when I remember my mother) without changing his identity (i.e. not having to become religious). This was a big step for Faizal to be able to place a boundary between his own identity and needs, and that of other members of his family. Although it was challenging for him and elicited strong feelings such as guilt and shame, he was better able to process this dilemma by using the diamond formulations and finding a compromise that worked for him at this time.

Case Study 6 – Ella

Ella is a 19-year old who identifies as a woman and uses she/her pronouns. Ella was referred to therapy due to the loss of her younger sister in a road traffic accident, and the subsequent trauma symptoms that were causing her significant distress. Ella presented with features of complex trauma in relation to the loss of her sister.

The initial intervention for Ella was trauma-focused CBT, using imaginal reliving and rescripting to reduce the distress associated with the road traffic accident. Ella reported that she and her family were travelling in a car which broke down as they were driving; as a result of this, a lorry hit their car from behind. As the lorry swerved to avoid the car, it impacted one side of the car more than the rest – the side where Ella's sister was seated. Ella's sister died in the accident, and Ella and her parents sustained significant injuries.

Phase 1

In the process of doing the trauma work, it became apparent that Ella's main difficulty was not with the traumatic event but the meaning she made of the death of her sister within the accident that is she was distressed by the meaning of the loss, not the meaning of the accident per se. The therapist expected Ella to blame the lorry driver or her father who was driving their car for the events that occurred – yet she consistently blamed herself. This deep level of self-blame seemed to be incongruous with the events which had taken place. It was also affecting Ella's day-to-day life significantly: she had stopped engaging with any activities at university, both academic and extra-curricular, was no longer playing sports or listening to music, and felt that she did not deserve to have any pleasant experiences or to be happy. When the LAG-FQ was administered, Ella had low scores – not because of the traumatic event – but because she blamed herself for what had happened.

The therapist asked Ella to speak a little bit about what it was like living with her sister. Ella gave an account of both good times and bad times, including arguments she and her sister had had. Ella was feeling upset with herself for not choosing the side of the car which ended up being hit the hardest and causing the death of her sister. Focusing on this version of events where she could have saved her sister was preventing her from considering the alternative – that if she had done so, she would have been the one to die. The therapist used a gently challenging approach to question Ella's meaning-making:

E: on the day of the accident, we had an argument about who's going to sit on which side of the car. if I had chosen that seat, I would have died instead of my sister.

T: okay, so then what would that be like for your sister?

E: I'm not sure. maybe similar to me.

T: okay. So this is a new learning. What do you think would be the best way to move forward with this idea?

E: I don't know what the best way would be.

The therapist was focused on exploring Ella's evidence for the self-blame. This strategy was chosen to help her become unstuck from the meaning she had made of the loss; it was necessary to think about this first, before moving on to considering changes and compromises since the loss.

Phase 2

From the conversation above, the therapist began to understand that Ella was caught in the bridging principle – looping over from blame to self-criticism within her rumination, and hence remaining stuck in the past. She had certain beliefs about how she "should" feel about the accident and the loss which were also contributing to the looping over. For example, Ella felt strongly that someone had to be held responsible for the accident, and she also believed that she was not allowed to feel better about losing her sister – even for a moment. These are both examples of ways in which the brain is trying to solve the problem and becomes caught – unable to find a solution and hence remaining frozen in the moment of the loss. Ella's self-criticism and self-blame were being continually triggered by the idea that she needed to hold someone accountable for the death of her sister; her mind could not find anyone else to pin the blame on, and hence it was turned inwards. The primary feeling that Ella was experiencing was a deep sadness for the loss of her sister, and she was presenting with secondary feelings of self-blame, anger directed towards the self, and guilt. Ella's way of coping with this self-blame was to detach, disconnect, or avoid reminders of her sister or reminders of the loss – for example, music and sports – which were things that her sister had also enjoyed.

The unintended consequence of this coping strategy was that it triggered the second loop in the bridging principle: when Ella disengaged from the loss as a way to seek relief from the self-blame, she felt marginally better – and this then became the trigger for the belief that she is not allowed to feel better at all. Therefore, she experienced even greater self-criticism and shame for allowing herself to become disconnected from the pain. This led to a renewal of rumination about the loss – bringing her back to the first loop of the bridging principle. In this way, Ella was completely stuck. The paradox of self was also at play here; Ella was valuing herself as less than others, and therefore consistently came to the conclusion that things would have been better off if she had been the one to die instead of her sister.

The therapist used a variety of questions over the course of multiple sessions to support Ella in becoming unstuck from this looping over: "What would it look like if you were feeling better?", "What would it look like if you had hope to be able to cope with this change?", "Are you willing to find out about the importance of your loss?" These questions intended to develop the potential for hope in Ella, and bringing into her awareness the idea that she may be able to live a life without her sister being in it.

Phase 3

In the third phase of intervention, the focus shifted to understanding what had changed in Ella's life since the loss, and trying to gradually increase her levels of activity and functioning. Ella felt that she could not possibly think about making changes to her life as doing so would dishonour the memory of her sister. Therefore, the therapist used Ella's strong bond with her sister as a way to talk about change in a way that was safer and more appropriate for Ella's needs.

T: if your sister was in your situation, what do you think would help her to recover?
E: I think it would help her if she started playing hockey again, hanging out with her friends, listening to music, and attending her lectures. At least then she has other things to focus on and not just think about the difficult stuff.
T: okay, so which of those are you willing to do?

Ella began to entertain the possibility of making changes to her routine, but she was struggling with motivation. Therefore, the therapist broke down tasks into 5-minute chunks. Ella agreed that she would try each activity for 5 minutes at least, and if she enjoyed it she would continue for as long as she wanted. If she didn't like the task, she would stop after 5 minutes. Ella started with listening to music, but she still felt a strong sense of blame – hence she chose to listen to her sister's music instead of her own. When Ella did this, she began to feel more of the here-and-now feelings of grief – the pain of losing her sister unexpectedly and her sadness in relation to this loss. This began the process of helping Ella to come unstuck from the frozen state she had been in since the accident.

Phase 4

Two sessions after this:

E: (laughing) my sister has poor taste in music.
T: okay, fair enough. Do you think your sister would have said the same about your taste in music?
E: yes definitely
T: so does that mean you need to keep listening to her music that you don't like?
E: no, I think it's okay for me to listen to my own music now.

As Ella slowly began to re-engage with activities that she enjoyed and gave her a sense of her identity outside of the loss, she began to slowly develop an acceptance of the changes in her life – even if she could not yet accept the loss itself. The focus in therapy was to explore what Ella could do to appreciate her own time and her interests – and to begin figuring out what the best compromise would be to live with the changes that had happened in her life since the loss. This process was made more challenging by the fact that Ella's parents were also experiencing significant grief and were not functioning well either. Ella reported many triggers for her sadness (and the resulting self-blame), such as seeing her sister's tooth-brush by the sink every time she used the bathroom. Ella's parents had not changed or moved anything in the family home, hence Ella's sister's belongings were constantly reminding her of the loss.

Phase 5

Through conversations in therapy, Ella was able to begin supporting her parents in gradually making changes at home. This included moving or removing her sisters' belongings so that they did not constantly trigger everyone's grief. This process was achieved by making a list of all the triggers which Ella was struggling with, and noting down how each trigger made her feel. The Emotion Log was used to scaffold this task, as Ella struggled to generate words to match her feelings.

T: and when you feel like that, what are the changes you notice?
E: I've lost my sister and I can't cope with that.
T: okay, so which of these triggers do you have control over and can change in some way?

This type of questioning was used in order to highlight not only triggers and feelings, but also the changes/impact of those triggers and feelings. Ella began to make links between triggers, feelings, and changes, which helped her to understand what she had choice and control over and the things that were outside of her choice or control. She began to take a more active role in exerting her choice and control across various aspects of her life in order to reduce her distress and the distress of her parents.

It is important to note that the trauma work was efficient enough to reduce distress, but the meaning attached to the events was debilitating; the meaning was related to the loss, not to the event itself. Some people might call this complex trauma, but the impact of loss is more long-standing than the trauma. The client may have fewer intrusions/reliving than before, but the rumination and obsessional-style thought patterns relating to the loss remain even after the trauma work has ended. Therefore, a step-by-step approach is needed where the therapist and client dig deeper and deeper to understand the layers of meaning-making and unpack secondary feelings from primary feelings. This helps to connect to the core pain that the person is experiencing and hence address functionality, rather than becoming stuck in the cycles which maintain presenting symptoms.

For Ella, this process led to the discovery of a conflict between her desires (motives) and her ideas about responsibility (values, right and wrong). Ella also felt that she had no choice or control over the things that had happened in her life and had generalised this to all future events: she felt hopeless and helpless in the face of a future without her sister. All of

Diamond Formulation

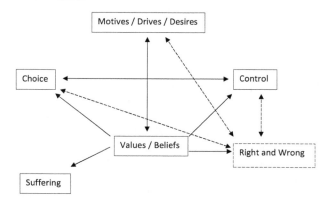

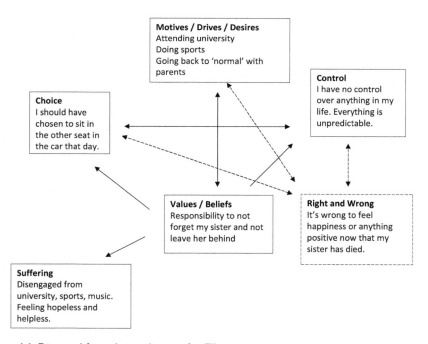

Figure 4.6 Diamond formulation diagram for Ella.

these experiences were related to Ella's motives and values: How can I move on when I'm guilty and need to be blamed? Her morals were saying: you were wrong, and that's why you have to feel guilty and you have to be punished.

Summary

Although these cases present a range of primary and secondary feelings, the main aim of intervention is about helping the person move forward from the problem that is unsolvable, and therefore stop them from looping over, or ruminating, or having intrusions. Which hopefully leads them to some form of resolution and acceptance.

There are occasions where the person's motivation is to not feel better. Sometimes you detect some secondary processes or secondary gain – where the client is not improving. It's not that common, but after all the work that's done, there are occasions where clients suggest that they would rather be upset or be sad. This is a form of self-punishment in response to the loss because they can't see any other way around it. In these instances, it's good to have a conversation about what stops the person from getting better. It's useful to have an open and honest conversation – is it something that's by choice? Or is it due to external or internal demand? The therapist needs to find out what might be the cause or justification, so that it can be discussed in a more open and honest way. There are common themes here relating to fear of what would that look like to move on without the deceased; they don't like the current state of being because they feel lonely and so they are at a loss – they need some direction; the worry or anticipation of what would it look like without the person that was there for them; or having the possibility of a dream in the future – I don't want to be alive/I don't want to take part in this process. This is usually framed in simple terms like "grief-stricken" or "it hasn't been enough time for the person to heal" or "they're just avoiding everything" – but we see that there's a function to the stuckness. This type of language is likely to make the person feel even more unable to find a resolution or compromise. Therefore bringing a compassionate lens to this dilemma and supporting the person in thinking about what might allow them to move forwards can be a good starting point for generating active changes in their functioning.

References

Arntz, A. (2012). Imagery rescripting as a therapeutic technique: Review of clinical trials, basic studies, and research agenda. *Journal of Experimental Psychopathology*, 3(2), 189–208.

Arntz, A., Tiesema, M., & Kindt, M. (2007). Treatment of PTSD: A comparison of imaginal exposure with and without imagery rescripting. *Journal of Behavior Therapy and Experimental Psychiatry*, *38*(4), 345–370.

Arntz, A., & Weertman, A. (1999). Treatment of childhood memories: Theory and practice. *Behaviour Research and Therapy*, *37*(8), 715–740.

Brockman, R. N., & Calvert, F. L. (2017). Imagery rescripting for PTSD and personality disorders: Theory and application. *Journal of Contemporary Psychotherapy*, *47*(1), 23–30.

Burnham, J. (2018). Relational reflexivity: A tool for socially constructing therapeutic relationships. In C. Flaskas, B. Mason, A. Perlesz, J. Byng-Hall, D. Campbell, & R. Draper (Eds.), *The space between* (pp. 1–17). Routledge.

Holmes, E. A., Arntz, A., & Smucker, M. R. (2007). Imagery rescripting in cognitive behaviour therapy: Images, treatment techniques and outcomes. *Journal of Behavior Therapy and Experimental Psychiatry*, *38*(4), 297–305.

Macaskie, J., Lees, J., & Freshwater, D. (2015). Talking about talking: Interpersonal process recall as an intersubjective approach to research. *Psychodynamic Practice*, *21*(3), 226–240.

Maslow, A., & Lewis, K. (1987). Maslow's hierarchy of needs. *Salenger Incorporated*, *14*(17), 987–990.

Mason, B. (2005). Relational risk-taking and the training of supervisors. *Journal of Family Therapy*, *27*(3), 298–301.

Chapter 5

Supervision

Given that this book focuses on working with loss and grief, the following chapter provides an overview of supervising work related to these experiences specifically. We build on foundational supervision approaches, methods, and techniques in order to provide a focus on the supervision of loss and grief in line with our model presented in the preceding chapters. Most supervision practices are derived from the training modality of supervisor and supervisee, styles of learning, therapeutic approaches, and individual characteristics. In this chapter, we provide an overview of the aims of supervision, oversight of caseload, efficacy of practice, stability of working with loss, internal and personal conflicts, and clinical skills or techniques.

Supervision in Practice

Good supervision requires adherence to "principles", for example the principles of cognitive behavioural therapy (CBT) supervision. There are multiple established and researched models of supervision available within the CBT practice, which readers are encouraged to read prior to engaging with this chapter (Bennett-Levy, 2006; Gordon, 2012; Milne & Reiser, 2012; Milne, 2017; Pretorius, 2006; Reiser & Milne, 2012).

The themes and approach to supervision would be dictated by the purpose and outcome of supervision the process. This may be clearly identified, for example there may be an agreement (supervision contract) on the structure, content, supervision style, and mode; be it CBT, compassionate, or ACT style of supervision. Others may have a less formal arrangement in place, but in all cases, we assume that the aim of supervision is to offer a platform for development and learning through a process that uses materials in support of learning such as, education, reflection, review of live recording, reports and case notes.

It is also vital for the supervision to have a clear direction, for example the identification of tasks. These could be identified or developed as part of the supervision contract, or incorporated into supervision itself. There are various other components to consider, such as ethical issues,

DOI: 10.4324/9781003214045-5

competencies, skills, attitude, and knowledge – and discussions regarding the process of exploring, developing, and challenging these areas need to be led by the supervisor.

It is envisaged that both supervisee and supervisor have utilised supervision regularly, and therefore are familiar with the basic structure and process, as well as their own core competencies and areas for further development. The intention of this section is to enable clinicians and their supervisors to become more attuned with the specific competencies required when undertaking work relating to loss. There is a specific need within loss work for clinicians to develop clarity in relation to their responsibilities and expectations, to develop the skills of reflection and reflexivity, and to create space for feedback and learning.

We encourage clinicians to spend considerable time in setting up the supervisory relationship and space, in order to have a more systematic, goal-directed, structured process that can usefully contribute to the development of an ethical, active, considerate, power-balanced approach to meet the needs of the supervisee. We feel that it is particularly important to focus on the interpersonal relationship between supervisor and supervisee and to develop a flexible approach that is both model-driven and fit for purpose in relation to the supervisee's personal and professional development needs.

Here we propose two specific frameworks for undertaking supervision: coaching and clinical supervision. The choice of approach is based on the supervisee's prior training, clinical experience, and their confidence and competence in relation to the work. A supervisor may need to shift between coaching and clinical supervision styles with supervisees based on their needs and the cases being discussed. We understand the whole process (which includes coaching and clinical supervision) to constitute "supervision" as a whole.

Coaching is typically used with supervisees who already have experience of the skills, knowledge, and techniques of the therapeutic approach and are able, confident, and willing to apply their existing skills in therapy. These supervisees require a coaching-based approach that focuses on fine-tuning already-learned skills. This may include small blocks to their creativity in clinical work or feeling apprehensive about applying their skills to a new/unfamiliar context. For example, a CBT therapist who has been practicing regularly, but has not worked with complex loss before would need a coaching-based approach in supervision. The intention is to support their professional development without undermining the supervisee or making them feel unable. The aim of coaching-based supervision is to increase the supervisee's confidence and competence to work with the client more efficiently. Coaching is about gently supporting and nurturing the person to come up with their own ideas about what to do next – which is the majority of clinicians who have been formally trained, are adhering to their training, and maintaining the standard of practice. Coaching-based supervision requires the supervisor to scaffold the supervisee by asking them to problem-solve based on their previous training and experience. For example, supervisors may ask "What do you think would be useful in this situation?", "What have you tried in the past which may be useful here?" and so on.

Clinical supervision, on the other hand, is an approach intended for supervisees who are at the beginning of their clinical journey and require a more nurturing and educational approach. These supervisees may not yet have the necessary basic skills of the therapeutic approach and hence require a greater emphasis on education, scaffolding, and modelling by the supervisor. Clinical supervision is therefore more focused on education and development of clinical skills and techniques. This type of supervision aims to support supervisees to become more clinically efficient.

Supervisees and supervisors would consider issues such as contracting during which the process, content, and mode of supervision would be agreed on. These are some additional components that would need to be considered within a supervision process:

- Supervision documentation or recording
- Supervision format, use of model or otherwise
- Case presentation, notes, live recording
- Formulation and case conceptualisation
- Good use of time
- Supervision question
- Ethical issues
- Performa for supervisors/supervisees
- Competency and responsibility as supervisor and supervisee
- Safe-practice
- How to choose a supervisor or supervisee
- Working with difficult people
- Legal issues
- Resource implications for you and your service

Supervisors and supervisees are also encouraged to consider a potential pitfall where information is withheld – for example, the supervisee does not feel able to share feelings of shame or hatred towards clients in the supervision space. These instances of withholding information may occur for a number of reasons, and we have labelled this act as a "Silent Dialogue" where the information is filtered by the supervisee in such a way that the supervisor is unaware of the depth or complexity of the supervisee's needs. Therefore supervisors are encouraged to make enquiries about the cases being discussed and to specifically ask for supervisees' experiences that have not yet been shared with the supervisor.

Other possible pitfalls within the supervision process would include matching of supervisors and supervisees. There are three possible positions: matched, overmatched, and unmatched. Overmatching occurs when a supervisee and supervisor spend a great deal of time socialising and avoiding engaging with the clinical materials, undermatching is when there is no connection or productive outcome from the supervision which could be due to a number of reasons and causes. Finally, the most efficient supervision process where both, supervisee and supervisor are matched, able to connect and work efficiently without avoidance or excessive demands, and with appropriate sharing of responsibilities.

We have utilised and modified supervision directives from Taylor et al. (2012) and presented these below with some elaboration of supervision format and content:

1 Clarify the supervision question.
   Aim for a clear question that will promote learning.
2 Elicit relevant background information.
   Keep it brief and structured, for example client problem statement, key points of history, formulation, and progress to date.
3 Request an example of the problem.
   This will usually include listening to a session tape extract.
4 Check supervisee's current understanding.
   This establishes their current competence and gives an indication of the "learning zone" where supervision should operate.
5 Decide the level or focus of the supervision work.
   For example, a focus on micro-skills, or problem conceptualisation, or on problematic thoughts and feelings within therapist.
6 Use of active supervision methods.
   Role-play, modelling, behavioural experiment, Socratic dialogue.
7 Check if the supervision question has been answered.
   Encourage the supervisee to reflect and consolidate the learning.
8 Format a client-related action plan.
   Formalise how the learning will be used within the therapy.
9 Homework setting.
   Discuss any associated development needs, for example reading-related literature or self-practice of a CBT method.
10 Elicit feedback on the supervision.
   Check for any problem in the supervision alliance or learning points for the supervisor.

Supervision with Loss

In addition to the above considerations, which relate to supervision more generally, we offer specific guidance for the supervision of loss. There are multiple layers to be aware of within the supervisory context such as the fluidity of the process, key learning outcomes, and dynamics between supervisor–supervisee and supervisee–client. There is a transaction of information from the client to the supervisor which occurs via the supervisee; the flow of information is mediated by the supervisee and hence they hold responsibility for the information that they receive, process, and share in both directions. For example, if a supervisee experiences something in the room with the client, they hold responsibility both to the client and to themselves to bring this to supervision. Supervisors, who naturally hold more power in this context, also hold responsibility to ensure that they create an open and safe enough space in supervision for supervisees to feel able to bring personal experiences and dilemmas. Supervisors can do this through modelling, scaffolding, and demonstrating their own vulnerability and reflexivity in the supervision space.

Alongside the above considerations for supervision that entails framework, style, content, and structure, we encourage additional features to be adopted when working with loss. We have identified the below list as components where adaptation would be encouraged:

- Open discussion around the impact of loss on both supervisee and supervisor within the supervision context (Proctor, 1986).
- Work in a systemic manner with regards to loss across time and explore relational content such as: dominance, verbal ability, attribution, and relation to the events, contingency and comparatives.
  - Dominance: When working with loss we have to have a construct of losses within the individual's life (might be single event, multiple events, etc.). This is in relation to the supervisee's experiences of loss. The supervisor needs to explore relational issues/factors/features – which are closely related to the power balance in the supervisory relationship. Sometimes there's a sense of vulnerability and sharing this information may make the supervisee feel less in control and create a position of power/dominance for the supervisor within that interaction. It is important for supervisors to be aware of this and actively work to reduce the impact of the power imbalance through their own openness and vulnerability.
  - Verbal ability: This refers to the supervisee's ability to articulate their experiences of loss or their ability to be able to contain and manage that interaction with the supervisor.
  - Attribution: How does the supervisee make attributions between their losses, their client, and the current relationship with their supervisor? This is influenced by their previous experiences of supervision. For example, losing previous supervisors would influence the current supervisory relationship through comparison. For example, trying to find a new supervisor who lives up to the previous one who has been lost.

- Relation to events: How do these factors influence the discussion about the client? And what previous events influence the way that the supervisee is engaging within the supervision space?
- Contingency: For example, if the supervisor or supervisee is not able to continue in the relationship (e.g. long-term sickness, death) – what is the contingency plan? This is a responsibility of both supervisor and supervisee – to discuss and decide on how they would proceed in these scenarios.
- Comparatives: transference and countertransference. For example, if a supervisee is listening to client's loss and comparing it to their own losses, and then bringing it to the supervision. As a supervisor, you have to be attuned to the difference between the supervisee's own experiences and what the client is sharing. This can also be noted by the supervisee when they're reporting their experiences, and the supervisor would be able to share some of their personal losses. So this idea of making comparisons between experiences occurs within the supervisory relationship, isomorphically to the supervisee–client relationship.

- The above could be restrictive or enabling pending the individual's and social ability and limitations.
- Impact on supervisee and supervisor following the discussion
- Self-referential material in supervision; this could be understood and explored in terms of difficulties within the transference and countertransference paradigm
- Issues with the clinician imagining/reliving the loss – and imagining how they would cope with the loss if it happened to them
- Exploration of anticipatory loss
- Learning objectives and direction of supervision
- Self-care: both supervisee and supervisor require self-care when working with loss and bereaved.

We borrow from an Eye Movement Desensitisation and Reprocessing metaphor here: therapy is part of a train journey that an individual is on. The therapist is standing outside the train and shouting at them what to do. As the train speeds up, the therapist continues with the conversation until the client can do it on their own. We are not in the process with the person – we are an observer who is only present temporarily. It is the same in the supervisory relationship – we can only support supervisees for a part of their journey as clinicians. Therefore, whilst we do the best that we can in the time that we have, we also need to remain compassionate to ourselves and our supervisees that the process won't be easy and it also won't be "perfect" or "complete". Just as the therapist navigates this dilemma with their client, the supervisor simultaneously navigates a parallel dilemma with their supervisee.

Summary

Within this section we have provided a brief account of supervision as it relates to working with loss, indicating primarily, a minimum requirement for supervision that includes identification of a supervision contract, clarity in role and responsibilities, identification of style of supervision, and agreeing on the content of supervision. In addition, issues such as silent dialogue and filtering were noted.

Supervision for loss would be considered as add-on to the established supervision model, with specific considerations for the impact of discussing and reflecting on loss for supervisor and supervisee. This may include reflecting on internal or external triggers for loss, and how they maintain or exacerbate distress in the clinician and supervisor. We believe that discussing the personal impact of working with loss on the clinician can support supervisees to engage with these experiences in a more empathic way, which would translate into their therapeutic relationship with the client. Open discussions in supervision about the role that loss plays for the clinician can improve their skills in reflection and reflexivity (Driscoll, 2006), and hence lead to greater confidence in working with loss and grief in therapy.

References

Bennett-Levy, J. (2006). Therapist skills: A cognitive model of their acquisition and refinement. *Behavioural and Cognitive Psychotherapy*, *34*(1), 57–78.

Driscoll, J. (2006). *Practising clinical supervision: A reflective approach for healthcare professionals*. Elsevier Health Sciences.

Gordon, P. K. (2012). Ten steps to cognitive behavioural supervision. *The Cognitive Behaviour Therapist*, *5*(4), 71–82.

Milne, D., & Reiser, R. P. (2012). A rationale for evidence-based clinical supervision. *Journal of Contemporary Psychotherapy*, *42*(3), 139–149.

Milne, D. L. (2017). *Evidence-based CBT supervision: Principles and practice*. John Wiley & Sons.

Pretorius, W. M. (2006). Cognitive behavioural therapy supervision: Recommended practice. *Behavioural and Cognitive Psychotherapy*, *34*(4), 413–420.

Proctor, B. (1986). Supervision: A co-operative exercise in accountability. In A. Marken & M. Payne (Eds.), *Enabling and ensuring: Supervision in practice* (pp. 21–23). National Bureau and Council for Education and Training in Youth and Community Work.

Reiser, R. P., & Milne, D. (2012). Supervising cognitive-behavioral psychotherapy: Pressing needs, impressing possibilities. *Journal of Contemporary Psychotherapy*, *42*(3), 161–171.

Taylor, K. N., Gordon, K., Grist, S., & Olding, C. (2012). Developing supervisory competence: Preliminary data on the impact of CBT supervision training. *Cognitive Behaviour Therapist*, *5*(4), 83–92.

LAG-FQ

We understand that experiencing a loss in our lives can have different levels of impact on our functioning and wellbeing, depending on various factors such as how recent the loss was, the relationship we had with the deceased, and the manner of their loss. Time is often not a healer, and it is a hugely personal journey that each of us goes through as we learn to rebuild our lives following a bereavement. We have developed this questionnaire as we would like to better understand people's journeys through the grieving process.

All data from this questionnaire will be stored and analysed in anonymised format in accordance with General Data Protection Regulation (GDPR) requirements, and regulations set by Information Commissioner's Office (ICO) confidentiality procedures. Please proceed with this questionnaire once you have understood the above information and if you give consent to the use of your data for the purposes of this academic work.

There are four preliminary questions prior to the main questionnaire.

*Required

1   What is your age? *
2   What is your gender identity? *
3   What is your ethnicity? (optional)
4   How long ago did you experience the bereavement? (if you've experienced multiple losses recently, please choose the most recent one) *

The following section contains 13 questions about key elements of daily life (e.g. emotional responses, memories, relationships, coping, etc.). We want to understand how each of these aspects of your life has been affected by the loss. Each question asks about how much that element of your life has changed, whether you spend a lot of time thinking about that part of your experience, how much those experiences get in the way of doing day-to-day activities, and to what extent you feel okay with any changes that have occurred since the loss.

Please be sure to answer the questions based on your experiences in the last month. We are trying to understand how you are processing your loss and how you relate to it in your daily life. There are no right or wrong answers to this questionnaire because we know that each person is unique and is affected differently by loss and grieving. Thank you for taking the time to complete this survey.

In the next section, you will be asked to rate each item on a scale of 1–5 in relation to these four factors. Please ensure that you answer questions based on the most recent bereavement you've experienced and based on your wellbeing in the last month.

1   In the last month, my social life (i.e. relationships with family, work, school, and social life): *

Tick all that apply.

	4 (not at all)	3	2	1	0 (very much)
My social life has changed significantly since the loss. (CH)					
I spend a lot of time thinking about how much my social life has been impacted by the loss. (MA)					
My ability to do the usual day-to-day social activities has changed since the loss. (CO)					
My social life has changed, but I can understand that it is a natural part of grieving and am okay with the changes. (AC)					

2   In the last month, my emotional responses (e.g. feeling numb, overwhelmed, anxious, low, avoiding things):

	4 (not at all)	3	2	1	0 (very much)
My emotional responses have changed significantly since the loss. (CH)					
I spend a lot of time thinking about how much my emotional responses have been impacted by the loss. (MA)					
My emotional responses impact on my ability to do day-to-day activities since the loss. (CO)					
My emotional responses have changed, but I can understand that it is a natural part of grieving and am okay with the changes. (AC)					

3   In the last month, the quality of my relationships (e.g. increased con-flict in relationships with others, overly involved in helping others):

	4 (not at all)	3	2	1	0 (very much)
The quality of my relationships has changed significantly since the loss. (CH)					
I spend a lot of time thinking about how much the quality of my relationships has been impacted by the loss. (MA)					
The quality of my relationships impacts on my ability to do the usual day-to-day activities since the loss. (CO)					
The quality of my relationships has changed, but I can understand that it is a natural part of grieving and am okay with the changes. (AC)					

4   In the last month, changes in my support networks (e.g. feeling distanced from social network and community support):

	4 (not at all)	3	2	I	0 (very much)
My support networks have changed significantly since the loss. (CH)					
I spend a lot of time thinking about how much my support networks have been impacted by the loss. (MA)					
The changes in my support networks impact on my ability to do the usual day-to-day activities since the loss. (CO)					
My support networks have changed, but I can understand that it is a natural part of grieving and am okay with the changes. (AC)					

5   In the last month, my ability to cope (e.g. lower tolerance for stress, feeling confused or disorganised due to stress, feeling unable to cope):

	4 (not at all)	3	2	I	0 (very much)
My ability to cope has changed significantly since the loss. (CH)					
I spend a lot of time thinking about how much my ability to cope has been impacted by the loss. (MA)					
My ability to cope impacts on my ability to do the usual day-to-day activities since the loss. (CO)					
My ability to cope has changed, but I can understand that it is a natural part of grieving and am okay with the changes. (AC)					

6   In the last month, my memories of the person I have lost, as well as memories of the loss itself (including experiencing intrusive memories in relation to the loss):

	4 (not at all)	3	2	1	0 (very much)
My memories of the person and the loss have changed significantly since the loss. (CH)					
I spend a lot of time thinking about my memories of the person and memories of the loss. (MA)					
My memories of the person and the loss impact on my ability to do the usual day-to-day activities since the loss. (CO)					
My memories of the person and the loss have changed, but I can understand that it is a natural part of grieving and am okay with the changes. (AC)					

7   In the last month, my view of myself (e.g. self-criticism, shame, guilt, and self-blame):

	4 (not at all)	3	2	1	0 (very much)
My view of myself has changed significantly since the loss. (CH)					
I spend a lot of time thinking about how much my view of myself has been impacted by the loss. (MA)					
My view of myself impacts on my ability to do the usual day-to-day activities since the loss. (CO)					
My view of myself has changed, but I can understand that it is a natural part of grieving and am okay with the changes. (AC)					

8   In the last month, my self-care (e.g. seeking comfort and reassurance from others, how much I am able to look after myself):

	4 (not at all)	3	2	1	0 (very much)
My self-care has changed significantly since the loss. (CH)					
I spend a lot of time thinking about how much my self-care has been impacted by the loss. (MA)					
My self-care impacts on my ability to do the usual day-to-day activities since the loss. (CO)					
My self-care has changed, but I can understand that it is a natural part of grieving and am okay with the changes. (AC)					

9   In the last month, my understanding of the impact of the loss (how much the loss has affected me):

	4 (not at all)	3	2	1	0 (very much)
My understanding of the impact of the loss has changed significantly since the loss. (CH)					
I spend a lot of time thinking about my understanding of the impact of the loss. (MA)					
Thinking about the impact of the loss affects my ability to do the usual day-to-day activities. (CO)					
My understanding of the impact of the loss has changed, but I can understand that it is a natural part of grieving and am okay with the changes. (AC)					

10   In the last month, my attitudes towards recovering from the loss:

	4 (not at all)	3	2	1	0 (very much)
My attitudes towards recovering from the loss have changed significantly since the loss. (CH)					
I spend a lot of time thinking about my attitudes towards recovering from the loss. (MA)					
My attitudes towards recovering from the loss affect my ability to do the usual day-to-day activities since the loss. (CO)					
My attitudes towards recovering from the loss have changed, but I can understand that it is a natural part of grieving and am okay with the changes. (AC)					

11   In the last month, my ability to differentiate between past, present, and possible future experiences:

	4 (not at all)	3	2	I	0 (very much)
My ability to differentiate between past, present, and future has changed significantly since the loss. (CH)					
I spend a lot of time thinking about how my ability to differentiate between past, present, and future has been impacted by the loss. (MA)					
My ability to differentiate past, present, and future affects my ability to do the usual day-to-day activities since the loss. (CO)					
My ability to differentiate past, present, and future has changed, but I can understand that it is a natural part of grieving and am okay with the changes. (AC)					

12 In the last month, my orientation to time (e.g. feeling overwhelmed by the past, believing I have no future):

	4 (not at all)	3	2	I	0 (very much)
My orientation to time has changed significantly since the loss. (CH)					
I spend a lot of time thinking about how my orientation to time has been impacted by the loss. (MA)					
My orientation to time affects my ability to do the usual day-to-day activities. (CO)					
My orientation to time has changed, but I can understand that it is a natural part of grieving, and am okay with the changes. (AC)					

13   In the last month, my spiritual and/or religious beliefs:

	4 (not at all)	3	2	1	0 (very much)
My spiritual / religious beliefs have changed significantly since the loss. (CH)					
I spend a lot of time thinking about how my spiritual / religious beliefs have been impacted by the loss. (MA)					
My spiritual / religious beliefs impact on my ability to do the usual day-to-day activities since the loss. (CO)					
My spiritual / religious beliefs have changed, but I can understand that it is a natural part of grieving and am okay with the changes. (AC)					

Scoring Guide

Sub-Scores (Each Out of 52):

Dimension	Score
Change (CH)	
Metacognitive awareness (MA)	
Coping (CO)	
Acceptance (AC)	
Total score (sum of all of the above)	

Total Functionality Score Ranges:

Degree of functionality	Range of scores
Low	0–52
Moderate	53–104
Moderately high	105–156
High	157–208

Feelings Log

Monday	Tuesday	Wednesday	Thursday	Friday	Saturday	Sunday

List of Feelings (taken from www.berkeleywellbeing.com/list-of-emotions.html):

Acceptance	Charity	Doubt
Admiration	Cheeky	Dread
Adoration	Cheerfulness	Driven
Affection	Claustrophobic	Dumbstruck
Afraid	Coercive	Eagerness
Agitation	Comfortable	Ecstasy
Agony	Confident	Elation
Aggressive	Confusion	Embarrassment
Alarm	Contempt	Empathy
Alarmed	Content	Enchanted
Alienation	Courage	Enjoyment
Amazement	Cowardly	Enlightened
Ambivalence	Cruelty	Ennui
Amusement	Curiosity	Enthusiasm
Anger	Cynicism	Envy
Anguish	Dazed	Epiphany
Annoyed	Dejection	Euphoria
Anticipating	Delighted	Exasperated
Anxious	Demoralized	Excitement
Apathy	Depressed	Expectancy
Apprehension	Desire	Fascination
Arrogant	Despair	Fear
Assertive	Determined	Flakey
Astonished	Disappointment	Focused
Attentiveness	Disbelief	Fondness
Attraction	Discombobulated	Friendliness
Aversion	Discomfort	Fright
Awe	Discontentment	Frustrated
Baffled	Disgruntled	Fury
Bewildered	Disgust	Glee
Bitter	Disheartened	Gloomy
Bitter sweetness	Dislike	Glumness
Bliss	Dismay	Gratitude
Bored	Disoriented	Greed
Brazen	Dispirited	Grief
Brooding	Displeasure	Grouchiness
Calm	Distraction	Grumpiness
Carefree	Distress	Guilt
Careless	Disturbed	Happiness
Caring	Dominant	Hate

Hatred	Moody	Restlessness
Helpless	Mortified	Revulsion
Homesickness	Mystified	Ruthless
Hope	Nasty	Sadness
Hopeless	Nauseated	Satisfaction
Horrified	Negative	Scared
Hospitable	Neglect	Schadenfreude
Humiliation	Nervous	Scorn
Humility	Nostalgic	Self-caring
Hurt	Numb	Self-compassionate
Hysteria	Obstinate	Self-confident
Idleness	Offended	Self-conscious
Impatient	Optimistic	Self-critical
Indifference	Outrage	Self-loathing
Indignant	Overwhelmed	Self-motivated
Infatuation	Panicked	Self-pity
Infuriated	Paranoid	Self-respecting
Insecurity	Passion	Self-understanding
Insightful	Patience	Sentimentality
Insulted	Pensiveness	Serenity
Interest	Perplexed	Shame
Intrigued	Persevering	Shameless
Irritated	Pessimism	Shocked
Isolated	Pity	Smug
Jealousy	Pleased	Sorrow
Joviality	Pleasure	Spite
Joy	Politeness	Stressed
Jubilation	Positive	Strong
Kind	Possessive	Stubborn
Lazy	Powerless	Stuck
Liking	Pride	Submissive
Loathing	Puzzled	Suffering
Lonely	Rage	Sullenness
Longing	Rash	Surprise
Loopy	Rattled	Suspense
Love	Regret	Suspicious
Lust	Rejected	Sympathy
Mad	Relaxed	Tenderness
Melancholy	Relieved	Tension
Miserable	Reluctant	Terror
Miserliness	Remorse	Thankfulness
Mixed up	Resentment	Thrilled
Modesty	Resignation	Tired

Tolerance
Torment
Triumphant
Troubled
Trust
Uncertainty
Undermined
Uneasiness

Unhappy
Unnerved
Unsettled
Unsure
Upset
Vengeful
Vicious
Vigilance

Vulnerable
Weak
Woe
Worried
Worthy
Wrath

Appendix C

Daily Log of Productive and Unproductive Activities

	Monday	Tuesday	Wednesday	Thursday	Friday	Saturday	Sunday
Productive activities							
Unproductive activities							

Daily Log of Rumination and Worry

	Monday	Tuesday	Wednesday	Thursday	Friday	Saturday	Sunday
Rumination							
Worry							

My Lifetime Values

Past values	Current values	Future values

Index

Lightning Source UK Ltd.
Milton Keynes UK
UKHW020646201222
414195UK00008B/56